HEAVEN

ROGER FERLO
editor

SEABURY BOOKS
An imprint of Church Publishing Incorporated, New York

Library of Congress Cataloging-in-Publication Data
Heaven / Roger Ferlo, editor.
      p.   cm.
Includes bibliographical references.
ISBN 978-1-59627-044-2 (pbk.)
1. Heaven—Christianity. 2. Heaven in literature. I. Ferlo, Roger, 1951– .
BT846.3.H43 2007
236'.24—dc22   2007000346

Printed in the United States of America.

Church Publishing, Incorporated
445 Fifth Avenue
New York, New York 10016

5 4 3 2 1

For my parents

CONTENTS

ACKNOWLEDGMENTS

CYNTHIA SHATTUCK first suggested the topic of heaven for this project, and has been its chief support, goad, trouble-shooter, and all-around guardian angel. One could not ask for a better editor, or a more loyal friend. I am grateful to all the writers who have contributed to this volume with such timeliness and grace, and want especially to thank Phyllis Tickle, Rick Moody, and Susan Wheeler for advice at strategic moments. For reasons beyond their control, Carolyn Forché and Darcey Steinke were not able to contribute essays to this book. Their early support and encouragement were instrumental in getting things started.

I am grateful to my colleagues, especially Dean Martha Horne, for the intellectual and spiritual hospitality that make Virginia Theological Seminary such a gracious place to work. Professor Judy Fentress-Williams steered me to the verse of the Negro spiritual in the essay that opens this collection, and Kathryn Lasseron offered both logistical support and an engaged reader's eye at a crucial juncture. I am also grateful to the monks of Mariya uMama weThemba Monastery in Grahamstown, South Africa, and to my colleagues and students in Grahamstown at the College of the Transfiguration, for hospitality and spiritual companionship as this project took final shape. In the end, as always, I owe my wife Anne Harlan and my daughter Liz Harlan-Ferlo more thanks than can be noted here.

Once more it is a case of maybe,
and once more maybes are the
essence of the situation.
— William James, "Is Life Worth Living?"
(delivered to the Harvard Young Men's
Christian Association, 1895)

Ev'rybody talkin' 'bout heav'n ain't goin' there.
— Negro Spiritual

MAYBE NOT, MAYBE SO

EDITOR'S INTRODUCTION
Roger Ferlo

NOT LONG AGO the television personality Barbara Walters aired a Christmas special on the topic of heaven, during which she asked an assortment of theologians, religious figures, and (perhaps inevitably in America) Hollywood celebrities about their hopes and expectations when challenged to imagine a heavenly Beverly Hills.

The responses she drew from people ranged all over the celestial map. The Dalai Lama, interviewed on location in the Himalayas, told Walters that the purpose of life is to be happy, and that you can accomplish that by "warmheartedness." A Muslim terrorist whom she interviewed in a high security Israeli prison assured her that "everything that is good is in the garden in paradise," and that "the Lord promised the martyr who lost his life and lost the world on earth, that he promised him these seventy-two women in paradise as honor, as respect for him." A Roman Catholic archbishop told her that "we're made for heaven." Asked about near-death experiences, after which many otherwise sensible people testify that they have had a glimpse of the heavenly landscape, one scientist speculated that the drop in oxygen level creates massive overactivity in the brain: "I think there

1

is a true transformation, but not because you've been to heaven." But in response, another scientist testified that "my near-death experience changed everything about me.... There is not a single experience on earth that could ever be as good as being dead."

What is it about heaven that prompts even the least religious people to speculate about the life to come?

The enormous popular response to Mitch Albom's *Five People You Meet In Heaven* and Alice Sebold's novel *The Lovely Bones,* about a murdered girl watching her family's story unfold from her vantage point in the afterlife, shows us how compelling, anguished, and yet hopeful a topic this can be. It furnishes rich material for television shows like *Touched By An Angel, Six Feet Under,* and *Dead Like Me,* but ironically not for sermons or serious theological comment, except in the most conservative of our pulpits. In spite of what the preachers say or refuse to say, thoughts of heaven in America seem to be overwhelmingly ecumenical, or at least more ecumenical than the churches where American Christians prepare themselves for the final transit. A *Newsweek*/Beliefnet poll, conducted about the same time as the Walters interviews aired, asked people whether or not a good person who doesn't happen to share their own religious faith could go to heaven. A whopping sixty-nine percent of respondents (including a surprising number of evangelical Christians) thought it could happen—that heaven was open to all comers, regardless of what church they belonged to, and even if they belonged to no church at all.

As compelling a topic as it is for ordinary people, heaven is largely ignored by our more serious religious thinkers. Liberal Christians especially tend to stress the "this-worldliness" of religious faith, seeking to downplay the invidious theology of punishment and reward that so often bedevils Christianity in America—the separation of sheep from goats and wheat from weeds, of who's in from who's out. This pastoral emphasis on matters of *this* world rather than of the world to come is understandable perhaps, considering the social injustices that surround us, and the emotional injuries so often inflicted by fiery preaching about heaven and hell. As the old spiritual wisely says, "Ev'rybody talkin' 'bout heav'n ain't goin' there." But theologians and preachers who, fearing the worst, avoid the topic of the afterlife end up marginalizing the subject of eternity, leaving thoughts of heaven to popular fiction and the talk shows—or to the punishing rhetoric of pulpit-pounding evangelists.

This book is a small attempt to break the silence—to imagine heaven anew. When we approached this group of writers—pastors, artists, historians, poets, teachers, therapists, novelists, spiritual guides—and asked them to write short, personal essays on the subject of heaven, we weren't sure what we would get, although we assumed there wouldn't be a lot of talk about angels and harps. One thing we discovered was that thoughts of heaven bring out the inner agnostic, even among the strongest believers. When it comes to traditional images of heaven, that mysterious place Up There, the typical reaction in these pieces is Maybe, Maybe Not. On reflection, this attitude is no surprise. How can you imagine or describe a place that is not-place, a time that is not-time? There's a huge risk in trying to talk about heaven with any integrity, especially in these credulous times, and it is not as if this were fresh new territory. To quote William James, that great American master of the Maybe in religious experience, "Much that commonly passes for spiritual self-seeking is only material and social self-seeking beyond the grave." Siding with James, one thing these writers make clear is that religious dogmas, baldly stated, cannot do heaven justice. And yet, in spite of their skepticism toward traditional views, in spite of their ambivalent stance of Maybe, Maybe Not, when faced with the prospect of heaven these writers share the strong desire to explore and pursue the Maybe So.

In a way, the theologians and preachers who avoid too
much heavenly talk get it right. Talk of heaven needs to be
talk of *this* world, but only if focusing on things as they are
leads us to probe the outermost edges of the here-and-now.
Only by considering closely the things of this world can we
have any clue about the things of the next. This is an ancient
insight, what the medieval theologians called the analogy of
being. It is the conviction that in the warp and woof of
God's creation we discern, if only by analogy or metaphor
or indirection, a glimpse of the divine beauty and the divine
splendor, what the poet T. S. Eliot called "a tremor of bliss, a
wink of heaven" *(Murder in the Cathedral).* So you will find
much talk in these essays of the world's beauties—of gardens
and banquets, of sculptures and wines, of erotic touch and
earthly loving. The sensuous spirit of the Song of Songs ani-
mates many of these pages, where analogies of heavenly
beauty can be discerned in works of art as diverse as Dante's
Purgatorio and Led Zeppelin's "Stairway to Heaven."

But you will also find talk here of devastating loss: the
death of a parent or a child, the aging of the body, a stint in
jail, the break-up of a marriage, a cancer diagnosis, a near-
death experience. Considering heaven afresh seems to chas-
ten our deeply-held fantasies of survival, and gives us
courage to brave the shadowlands of our own impending
and inevitable losses. It looks like we put off thinking of
heaven until we absolutely have to, until we halt before a
perilous threshold that we have no choice but to cross. It is
no accident that the one writer mentioned most often in
these essays is Dante, that master of shadowlands and thresholds and stairways to heaven. In the face of loss, like Dante
we try to imagine heaven as a region of redeemed unlike-
ness, a vast reunion tent, a many-roomed house where perilous thresholds no longer separate us from our better selves,
and our better selves from God and our neighbor. It is a
crowded place, packed with relatives and co-workers whom,
by some mysterious act of grace, we no longer need either

to hate or to mourn. To imagine such a heaven is to imagine a place free of the disorder and disillusions that mar our feeble attempts at loving—loving not only our enemies, as Jesus so famously demanded, but also loving our sorry selves, our troubled souls and aching bodies.

You will find that most of these writers possess strong religious commitments, and many of them display a deep love of ritual. You will not find much talk of heavenly judgment—sheep and goats mingle pretty freely in the heavenly pastures imagined here. Eternal punishment for sin and eternal reward for the righteous do not seem to fire these writers' imaginations, perhaps because that brand of theology has set so many destructive fires in the past, and no doubt will continue to do so, needing no encouragement from any of us. Nonetheless, you will find hints and shadowings here of powerful scriptural visions—of Ezekiel's fiery chariot and the ancient Temple rebuilt, of gardens and vineyards restored, of what Peter Hawkins calls, with John's Revelation in mind, the jewel box of the Heavenly City in which every tear is washed away. Liturgies and rituals of passage emerge in these writers' religious practices as dress rehearsals for the real thing, celebrating the analogy of being by way of our own earthly senses—with graceful movement, sweet smells, lavish color, deep-toned sound, and a foretaste of the heavenly banquet in the bread and wine even of a simple communion service. In imagining heaven, we do the best we can with what we have, in the strong conviction that the things of this world carry within them the sacred lineaments of the things of the world to come.

As we talk of heaven this way, this book begins to describe what might be seen as the re-traditioning of religious life in America. What you are about to read is a foray into a post-modern way of approaching heaven. As is often the case, post-modernity begins to look a lot like pre-modernity—a restoration of ancient images and liturgical practices that had once been thought outmoded by the empirical certainties of the modern age. All this is a fancy way of saying that, in talking of heaven, there are not a lot of certainties. In the end, we don't know anything. We would be greater fools than we already are if we thought we did. So we pool our guesses. That heaven *is* is for many of us a deep and haunting conviction. What heaven is, and how it is what it is, not even the mystics can tell us. When it comes to heaven, we are grasping at straws.

But we are not on our own. Others have been there before us, and the promise of heaven, however much shadowed by our own fears and fallings off, remains a promise worth remembering, if only for the sake of those who have gone before. It takes some measure of courage in these contentious days to clear the old paths and sweep the stairways clean. What counts most in the end is a holy paradox. In directing our thoughts toward matters heavenly, we find ourselves grounded more firmly in the essential matters of earth.

LEAVING MYSELF BEHIND
Barbara Brown Taylor

A COUPLE OF WEEKS ago on my way to school, I saw a stunned cardinal clinging to the shoulder of the road. I pass so much roadkill on this stretch of highway that I often avert my eyes, but the flash of red was impossible to miss. I knew the cardinal was alive because he was still crouching upright instead of lying on his side. Pulling over as soon as I could, I turned on my emergency flashers and walked back to where he was sitting dazed as a drunk who knew better than to try and walk. His eyes were open, but he did not even blink as I leaned down to pick him up. Trying not to frighten him, I laid him in the little hammock I made for him in the hem of my blouse.

Back in the car, he lay perfectly still as I cranked the engine and pulled into traffic again. For the next two miles I could feel him in my lap, light as a leaf. I wondered where he thought he was. I wondered if my smell distressed him more than his encounter with the windshield that had ruined his day. Then, just as I was turning into the parking lot, he gave a loud squawk and burst back to life. I put one hand on him to keep him from flying in my face. He yelled as if I were strangling him, as if I were pulling out his toenails one by one. I parked as quickly as I could and found a suitable bush. The moment I opened my hand, he scuttled away from me, heading so deep into the bush that all I could see was a patch of red. When I went back later to check on him, he was gone.

I do this all the time. Once I picked up an odd little turtle that was stranded on the yellow centerline. When I got it back into the car, I realized it was a baby snapper. A couple of minutes later, it too burst back to life, racing over the front seat of my car looking for something to latch onto with its strong little jaws. I managed to reach Lake Demorest without losing any chunks of flesh, cupped the turtle between my two empty shoes, and released it into the water with an apology to the ducks whose ducklings the snapping turtle would one day eat.

In my life so far, I have rescued more creatures than I can count. From smallest to largest, they have included red-bellied spiders, Monarch caterpillars, hummingbirds, garter snakes, field mice, voles, lab rats, chipmunks, screech owls, squirrels, chickens that have fallen off chicken trucks, injured raccoons, orphaned opossums, stray cats, dogs, llamas headed to the slaughterhouse, and horses too lame to ride. None of them ever asked to be rescued, and none of them ever said thank you. It is entirely possible that they were never meant to be rescued, and that I thwarted the divine plan by subverting their fate.

Once they recovered, I never saw most of them again, but one of my favorite fantasies of heaven includes a reunion with them. In this dream, they are all fat and happy. They are furthermore all getting along. The birds are no longer eating the caterpillars. The dogs are no longer savaging the raccoons. I do not know what they eat in heaven, but they are not eating one another, any more than I am eating them. Having made it to the peaceable kingdom, we are healed of the appetites that once made us "natural" enemies. We are no longer smart animals or dumb, separated from one another by the number of our legs or the kinds of songs we sing. We are all God's creatures, enjoying our full communion with one another at last.

All in all, I do not spend much time thinking about heaven. In the first place, my mortal mind is not fitted to contemplate eternity. In the second place, I know too many believers whose investment in heaven has cheapened their commitment to earth. In the third place, it seems presumptuous of me to speculate on what scripture has left vague. And yet I am also aware that I do not spend much time thinking about heaven because my life on earth is very good. If I were living in a small cell at Guantanamo, or trying to feed children in a Sudanese refugee camp, I imagine that I would spend a great deal more time thinking about heaven, since my life on earth would more closely resemble hell.

Most people I know seem to think of heaven as compensatory. Whatever is missing here will be present there. Those who have endured war will know peace. Those who have suffered want will have plenty. Those who have been broken will be made whole. In this sense, heaven is essential both for divine justice and compassion, for heaven is where God's purpose will be fulfilled, and all people shall see it together. This is more or less what scripture promises, and what my Episcopal tradition teaches as well, yet it does not exhaust my curiosity about what comes next.

That *something* comes next seems likely to me, although I would gladly admit that I have no certainty about what it is. People I trust speak of seeing through the veil to the life beyond death. I have sat with dying people often enough to watch them become translucent toward the end. Plus, my sense of the communion of the saints is so strong that I have never in my life been lonely. Even when I cannot hear them speaking any language I understand, the very air is thick with their presence. This could be my imagination. What if God's imagination is where heaven exists?

I suppose my greatest curiosity about the afterlife is whether I will continue to be me. I want to continue being me, of course. I want not only to see all of those creatures that I have rescued through the years; I also want to see the loved ones whom I have lost. I want to lay my head on Grandma Lucy's lap again. I want to shell field peas with Fannie Belle and listen to Schubert with Earl. The problem with this scenario is that it turns heaven into my perfect version of earth, with a perfect me in the middle of it. As appealing as this is, it strikes me as an underutilization of God's gifts.

Since ecstatic union with God is my best idea of heaven, I think I have to be ready to let myself go—literally, I mean. I think I have to entertain the possibility that joining God in heaven may mean surrendering everything I hold dear on earth, including my me-ness, in order to be made entirely new. In Christian terms, I think I really do have to die, and be willing to leave the rest to God.

When my father lay dying several years ago, I hardly left his room for the last two weeks of his life. This gave me a lot of time to think about what was happening to him, and where he might be going. He had lived a good life too—so good that he was clearly reluctant to leave. This man loved fine food, fine arts, fine clothes, and fine cars. He loved his work. He loved to travel. He loved his friends and his family. Subsisting now on nothing but a few drops of water squeezed into his mouth every couple of hours, he hung on to all these loves like a badger.

As people filed in to pay their last respects, I asked them please not to hold him back. He was so sedated that it was difficult to know how much he took in, yet even after the visitors had slowed to a trickle, he hung on. One friend of his consulted a psychic to visit my father "in the in between" in order to discover what was going on.

"Wow," the psychic's report came back, "is he ever stubborn. I don't know when I have met such a stubborn spirit."

One Sunday afternoon I lay my head on my father's pillow so I could whisper in his ear. "I think I finally get what's taking you so long," I said. "You're having to let it all go, aren't you? All the places you haven't traveled yet, all the places you've been. Your first girlfriend, your favorite chair, your prize students, your grandsons." I was crying now. "Everything that makes you you, you're having to let go now. Oh, Poppa, I don't know how you can do it. It has to be *so hard*."

He died at three that afternoon. After the undertaker had taken my father's body, I lay down in his hospital bed. I fully expected him to be there in spirit somehow, but when I got up, the room was dark and empty as a tomb. Around the same time the next day, I was thinking of him when I felt him take off like a rocket. For about three seconds, a wave of pure bliss washed through my body. Then I knew my father was *gone*. He had left all his Earl-ness behind.

Maybe he got it all back again when he arrived where he was going, or maybe he discovered that "me" was too small a box for who he became in God. I may never know, but ever since then I have become less attached to my beliefs about heaven. In their place, I am cultivating what I hope is radical trust in God. In the face of all that I do not know about heaven, I am still willing to go where God wants me to go and to be what God wants me to be, even if I have to leave me behind.

One enduring sense I have is that everything will be revealed in the hereafter. In the words of the old Anglican collect for purity, heaven exists in the presence of the God "unto whom all hearts are open, all desires known, and from whom no secrets are hid." I think of this when I say something disloyal about someone who is not present, or when I try to hide the truth about myself from people whose illusions flatter me. If all of this will be perfectly transparent by-and-by, why not prepare for that by practicing transparency now?

Of course I also harbor the hope that if I have managed to do or be any good for God, that will be transparent too. I am embarrassed to admit that, but as someone who has spent my whole life confessing my sins, the prospect of being allowed to discover what I might have done right in this world sounds like heaven to me.

If it is true that most of us give what we want to get, then in the end my highest hope for heaven is simply to be rescued when my time comes—plucked from the roadside where I have fallen, struck dumb by all there is to love and grieve in this world—and gathered into God's own safety, whatever that turns out to mean. I am willing to forego the details, as long as I know whose lap I am in.

THE HAPPINESS OF HEAVEN
Robert A. Orsi

THE PLAYGROUND OF my Catholic school in the north Bronx in the early 1960s was a cruel and vicious place. It seems silly to say this in the face of the much greater horrors of the world, but the playground was real and immediate to me then, and it was bad and dangerous ground. I watched a circle of boys one afternoon piss on a classmate, a much-tormented child they had pushed to the ground at their feet. Where were the nuns, who at other times seemed to be everywhere? The boy writhed and screamed under the hot flow, and then pulled himself up dripping and foul to make his way home alone under the shadows of the elevated train tracks on White Plains Road. Two children in particular, male cousins from the forbidding neighborhood behind the church, whirled through the playground before and after school every day, punching and howling, tearing at other children's clothes and faces and hair.

In the revised 1941 edition of the *Baltimore Catechism,* the compendium of Catholic doctrine in the form of questions and answers that parochial school children in the United States, including those pissing and being pissed on in the Bronx, were made to memorize word for word in the mid-

dle years of the twentieth century, the word "heaven"
appears for the first time in the fourth question. "What must
we do to gain the happiness of heaven?"

With the other good boys I mostly accepted the playground's savagery with the stoic resignation of doomed children as a normal part of everyday life. But sometimes it
became too much for me. Then, if I could get away without
being seen, which would have drawn the feral cousins
shrieking down on me, I slipped into church through the
side door that opened onto the playground. I was an altar
boy and I knew my way around the back hallways of the
church. I crossed the sacristy where the vestments and chal-
ices and wine for Mass were stored, slipped behind the main
altar, past the choir stalls where the friars chanted the morning office, to a side chapel dedicated to Saint Anthony of
Padua. The chapel glowed from within with a deep flicker-
ing red light that came from the tiers of votive candles burning before the saint in need and thanksgiving. The old
women of the neighborhood lit the candles, and these old
women, dressed in black and murmuring over thick prayer
books and beads, were mostly the only people I ever saw in
the chapel in the middle of the day. The place smelled
sweetly of incense and hot wax.

The answer is, "to gain the happiness of heaven we must
know, love, and serve God in this world."

The blood pounded in my ears in the chapel's immense
silence until I calmed down and my eyes adjusted to the
smoky darkness and then the playground's grip eased on my
heart at last. A statue of Saint Anthony, in brown Franciscan
robes with the baby Jesus in his arms, stood in the front of
the chapel. Behind them was a fresco, darkened and glazed
by the years of candle smoke and heat, that showed two long
lines of men and women making their way toward the open

and glowing gates of heaven in the distance up ahead of them. If you stood up close to the wall at either side of the fresco you'd be in the line yourself. The drone of the women's prayers went on and on.

Question 186 of this edition of the catechism near the very end of the book asked, "Who are rewarded in heaven?" The answer was, "Those are rewarded in heaven who die in the state of grace and have been purified in purgatory, if necessary, from all venial sin and debt of temporal punishment; they see God face to face and share forever in His glory and happiness."

A tall king in a great red cape with ermine piping and a golden crown walked alongside a man in dirty miner's gear. A soldier in a khaki uniform and high, laced brown boots, with a flat World War I helmet tucked under his arm (a detail that completely captured my boyhood imagination), was illuminated by the light pouring out of heaven's gates. Children skipped along holding hands. There were costumes from different periods of history and different parts of the world, and I vaguely remember a slender woman in a slinky, clinging dress. (Is this possible? The mural was covered over many years ago with thick coats of yellow paint so it is impossible now to check this odd memory. Maybe she was a Roman martyr, Saint Perpetua or Saint Felicitas, or maybe she is a figment of my early erotic fevers.) A fellow in a sharp 1930s gray suit and fedora strode along confidently on the road to heaven. I thought he looked like Bud Abbott of Abbot and Costello.

The work that heaven does in culture seems clear enough. Heaven grounds the realness of the otherwise contingent worlds that we humans struggle to make for ourselves in the face of nothingness, chaos, and death. Our short lives acquire not only purpose but also grandeur and drama against the

horizon of sacred history, the story that goes from the ori-
gins of the world to its end. Heaven absorbs the handful of
human years into its infinity. The time of societies is likewise
short and in the shadow of transience and death all the creations of human communities are weak and vulnerable. But
with heaven's sanction these fragile entities—the rightness
of a nation's choices, what is permitted sexually and what is
not, the guarantee of truth in a court of law, a ruler's authority, and so on—take on solidity and meaning. The anticipation of heaven's reward gives weight and inevitability to
moral choices—why shouldn't I do this, why should I do
this—they otherwise lack. "Heaven be my witness," people
say when they want to be trusted. Those who deny the
sacred order are cast out as evil; they are seen as making a
pact with the forces of disorder and destruction. Against
them the most monstrous things have been done in the
name of heaven. The sweet by-and-by when we will all be
united and there will be no more pain and we will see the
face of God has been called on to compensate for endless
suffering and injustice on earth. Those who assent to the
sacred order are rewarded in heaven. Heaven is the dullest
and most obvious of all religious phenomena.

In a special illustrated children's edition of the *Baltimore
Catechism* published in 1944 there is a set of "study exer-
cises" after the first seven catechetical questions that includes
the following: "5. The happiness of heaven continues
f_____. 6. To gain the happiness of heaven we must s____
God. 7. To gain the happiness of heaven we must k___ God.
8. To gain the happiness of heaven we must l___ God."
Further on there is a game: *"Put a ring around the names of the
boys and girls who serve God by doing what they know will please
Him."* Among the choices for children to think about are:
"3. Michael is lazy and is always late for Sunday Mass. 5.
John does not play in the busy street. 6. William is good to
the poor. 9. Gertrude cheats when playing games."

I asked a group of men in their forties and fifties in rural Nebraska, all graduates of Catholic schools, how they had understood heaven as children. "I thought that it would be like a time machine, basically," one of the men told me, "where you could get there and you could go back and see what the old West was like, or back in your own time, or you could go way ahead and just check everything out. All of this stuff that you wanted to see and investigate, that you wanted to know what it was like...just see all the things that you, you know, wondered about." Another man in the group added, "I had the idea also that all of those things would be revealed, all the questions I had. And I—I think I got that from some of my teachers, but also my mom, because when I had questions and asked her, 'Well, that's one of the mysteries that you never know until we die.'"

"I loved reading history," another man in the conversation said, "and I loved reading the lives of the saints and so I was looking forward to meeting some of them that I'd read about, like meeting Abraham Lincoln and George Washington and meeting Saint Patrick and seeing the angels." Heaven was a place, the men agreed, where people would be reunited with their dead friends and relatives, even those they had never met, the grandparents or parents or siblings who had died before they were born. "I remember when I was really young," one of the men said, "I lost a friend and my parents explained to me that someday" he would see his friend in heaven. "Nothing but the good times," he went on, "we'd be riding Shetlands together."

Before my mother died of cancer, before we even knew she was sick, my father retired from his work as a machinist and began volunteering at a cancer hospice in the north Bronx. His job there was to bring people whatever small treats they wanted during the day—chocolates, milkshakes, cigarettes, newspapers—and in the time they were in the hospice,

which could be several weeks or a couple of days, many
patients got to know my father well. They liked him. He
chatted in Italian with the people from the old neighborhood. "You never know who's going to show up there!" my
father exclaimed to me once. One old man who had been
a chef explained to my father how to cook a real *marinara*
sauce. "No onions!" He insisted my father understand and
accept this. *"Never* onions in *marinara* sauce!!" People
wanted my father to meet their children and grandchildren
when they came to visit. They told him about the lives they
had lived, very short lives for some, twenty or thirty years,
or less. My father complimented the women on how good
they looked. Many people waited to die for the days he was
there. My father figures that in the years he spent at the hospice he met several hundred people who died, some of them
holding his hand, and he anticipates that they will all be
there to greet him in heaven when his time comes. He quit
his volunteer job to stay home and take care of my mother
who was dying of colon cancer.

The man who imagined riding Shetland ponies in heaven
with his friends had a sister named Maureen who died in
her early twenties of leukemia, when he was just eleven
years old. "My sister went directly to heaven," he told me. "I
mean, I couldn't see she ever did wrong." Maureen was the
oldest of eighteen children, much loved by her younger siblings and by her parents, who simply could not accept the
fact of her death. They had denied the reality of her illness
until the very end. Soon after Maureen's death, her mother
began telling the other children that one day the church was
going to recognize their oldest sister as a saint. She stored
Maureen's things in attic to have ready for relics after her
daughter's canonization. "So I felt she went to heaven,"
Maureen's youngest brother went on, "and I felt if she's in
heaven that I can talk to her and that I can ask her for help."

"Do me the kindness to come here everyday for a fort-
night," the apparitional figure at Lourdes asked the young
girl, Bernadette, kneeling before her, and then she said, "On
my part, I promise to make you happy, not in this world but
the next." I take this translation of the words of Bernadette's
Lady in White from a "playlet" for Catholic children by
Sister Mary of Grace, C.D.P., published in the *Catholic School
Journal* in October 1934.

The wound in my mother's side was raw and open, "meaty"
is how my father describes it, "like an organ." "Aren't you
happy," my mother asked him when she came out of the
anesthesia, "that I don't have the tumor anymore?" and he
didn't have the heart to tell her that the tumor was inoper-
able and that the doctor had had to do an emergency
colostomy. When the doctor told her, my mother shrugged
her shoulders and said, "Well, what are you going to do?"
Every day my father cut the little patch that fit over the
opening, dressed it, and attached a new bag to his wife's side.
He assured her there was no smell. "You lose all dignity," my
mother told him once as he was cleaning her, but my father
says it never bothered him to do this. Every night she took
out her teeth and gave them to my father to clean. "Your
mother was spunky right to end," my father says. She chased
him out of the bathroom so he wouldn't watch her taking
her teeth out.

"I remember very vividly the Q and A from the *Baltimore
Catechism*," a woman named Marlene in her early fifties
who grew up in a Colorado town "where we had a lot of
military bases" told me. "'Is there salvation outside the
church?' Answer: 'No, there's no salvation outside the
church.' And I thought, 'Okay, that takes care of my mom,'"
who wasn't Catholic. Marlene married a Catholic man and
raised her children in the church. When her oldest daughter, a talented and popular athlete, died suddenly and unex-

pectedly in her early twenties from an undiagnosed heart
condition, Marlene said, "Our faith was definitely the rock
of our lives." She and her husband chose to live in a kind of
intentional community with other Catholic families gathered around a conservative parish in Phoenix, Arizona.

Recalling the time when his daughter died, Marlene's
husband said, "We endure. It's something we endure and . . .
as we go through life together that indeed there is this wonderful mystery of us being, all eventually being [called] to
great sacrifice and our own life is not our own. Ultimately,
everything we think we have, and have been given, is going
to be given back again." In the autumn when she was a
child, Marlene helped her father rake the leaves in the backyard, "and we were burning them . . . and I remember
watching that flame, that fire, and thinking of hell." She
thought "especially about my mom," who was going to hell
because she was not Catholic. Marlene no longer believes
this, but it took many years for her not to see her mother in
the flames.

My mother stopped eating in her last month. My father sat
next to her bed, begging her to take a spoonful of ice cream
or applesauce. I tell him that he was very brave during that
time, and he answers me, "How was I brave? She was the
one who was brave." Then she lost the strength to make the
short distance in their apartment from her hospital bed in
the living room to the bathroom. One night she fell under
the sink. No longer as strong as he was when he worked in
the factory, my father knelt beside her, unable to lift his wife
from the floor. "Help me," he said to her, "help me lift you."
The two of them struggled until she was upright and he
could maneuver her into the old beach chair my father used
to push my mother around the apartment's linoleum floors.
She didn't want to sit in a wheelchair.

"And he who was sitting on the throne said, 'Behold, I make all things new!' And he said, 'Write, for these words are trustworthy and true'" (Rev. 21:5). Catholic theologian Romano Guardini, reflecting on Saint John's vision of heaven, understands it as the awakening "to the full maturity of love." The whole creation is included in this love. "The huge heart of the God-man, which once lived in terrible solitude, 'abandoned' by all, even by the Father, will triumphantly enfold all things that will exist in it, manifesting its radiance everywhere. Everything will be transparent, luminous."

"We used to sit there at night and talk," my father told me one afternoon, two years after my mother's death, when we were alone together. My parents' marriage was tumultuous, although I am probably the least capable of judging because I experienced it all as a child. Their fights were terrifying to me. They fought often, bitterly, both for reasons they could name and for others that were buried deep in their histories and in their parents' and grandparents' lives. Sometimes the neighbors called the police. These huge men with guns and ballpoint pens and pads creaking in leather holders on their wide hips sat in the kitchen with my parents drinking coffee in the sudden and shocking calm that had descended. But at the end of my mother's life they found themselves at peace. She asked my father, "Do you think it's all true?" Is there anything to it? Did he really think so? "Is what true?" I asked him. "Heaven," he said, "is there really a life after death?" "Did Mom doubt this?" "You have to wonder," my father said. "I don't know. Who really knows?"

"And I heard a loud voice from the throne saying, 'Behold the dwelling of God with men, and he will dwell with them. And they will be his people, and God himself will be with them as their God. And God will wipe every tear from their eyes. And death shall be no more; neither shall there be mourning, nor crying, nor pain any more, for the former things have passed away'" (Rev. 21:3–4).

I wonder as a historian and a scholar of religion about my mother's doubt. Was this evidence of the breakup of Catholic certainty in the late modern world, after the vast changes in Catholic life following the Second Vatican Council? My mother fits a certain profile of change. She was born on New York's Lower East Side, lived most of her life in the Italian north Bronx, but died in a working class suburb populated by others who had left the old neighborhoods, as she had done too, sadly and reluctantly, twenty years before, when drugs and murder had finally taken over. She worked as a secretary at the Jesuits' Fordham University, where in the 1960s, at the time of the Second Vatican Council, she got caught up in the excitement of the church's liturgical and social transformations. My mother used to say that half the nuns and priests at Fordham who left to marry each other had met in our living room over macaroni and red wine. She was a eucharistic minister for the Fordham University chapel. Anthropologist Ellen Badone, who has studied the attitudes of contemporary Catholics in Brittany toward the afterlife, found that since Vatican II heaven has faded in its vividness and urgency. One man told her, "Now there aren't any more fires in hell. They've installed central heating! The road to heaven used to be rocky and difficult. Now it has been paved and they're going to take us there by car!"

Others in the contemporary world do not have such doubts as my mother's, the religious leaders who call down the wrath of their gods on people they don't like and who know with complete conviction that heaven is for them and for their fellows. "Heaven" in the mouths of these men and women comes closer to the word's predictable meanings, the horizon of certainty that elevates human prejudice and power to the authority of the sacred. My mother was never very political, so her notions of the afterlife lacked the borrowed assuredness of political rage and social hate. Still, there may be a religious historical context for my parents' late night conversations.

What is heaven, then? Guardini continues, "Interior and exterior will be no more, only the presence of the reality that is love. Love is the permanent state of creation. Identity of interior and exterior: that is heaven."

But I've also wondered, thinking about the two of them holding hands in the room that had become my mother's hospice and would soon be the room she died in, whether there is something in the constitution of the human and of culture that the more real something is to us the more drawn we are to doubt it. What is not doubted is not experienced as really real, so those who do not doubt must look elsewhere for the means to make their worlds real for themselves and others, to destruction, violence, and enmity. But the closer humans move to what is real to them the more their doubts and uncertainty rise, until, inevitably, they find themselves asking others to come near, to help them not to resolve but to hold the doubt and uncertainty with them. Heaven in this case becomes not the dull guarantor of desperate human pretension or the ground of meaning but the limit of knowing and an invitation to conversation and communion at the extremity of life.

People who needed something from Saint Anthony lit the candles that burned in front of his statue. I lit candles there too when I was a boy. We wanted some sorrow to pass, or to ask the saint to help with a terror we could no longer bear on our own, or with a family crisis that wouldn't end. The banks of candles burning before the saint held the neighborhood's inner history and made its needs visible in flame.

Outside the chapel's windows brakes on city buses hissed, the el train rumbled above Webster Avenue, and children in the playground yelled and screamed at each other. In the smoking light of the votive candles the mural of heaven shimmered and darkened. The boy who was pissed on in the playground grew up to become, among many other things, an astrologer.

My daughter Claire edited earlier versions of this essay and guided it to its final form. The essay is dedicated to my son Anthony, my mother's namesake, who was born just after her death.

Bibliographical Notes

The catechetical questions about heaven come from *A Catechism of Christian Doctrine, Revised Edition of the Baltimore Catechism, No. 2* (Paterson, N. J.: St. Anthony Guild Press, 1941), 1 and 36. My gratitude to the Boston College Library Liturgy and Life Collection for letting me see this particular old edition.

The children's quiz about heaven appears in *The Illustrated Revised Edition of Baltimore Catechism, No. 1* (New York and Chicago: W. H. Sadlier, Inc., 1944), 3–4.

The Lady's request to Bernadette at Lourdes is taken from Sister Mary of Grace, C.D.P., "Apparitions of Lourdes—Playlet for December 8," *Catholic School Journal,* vol. 34 (December 1934): 287–289, from page 288.

The comment made by one of Ellen Badone's sources about the paved road to heaven is quoted in *The Appointed Hour: Death, Worldview, and Social Change in Brittany* (Berkeley: University of California Press, 1989), 230.

Guardini reflects on the book of Revelation in the last chapters of his work *The Lord* (Chicago: Henry Regnery Company, 1954), quotations from pages 530–531. Revelation ends, Guardini points out, "in the simple intimacy of the name once given God on earth, 'I, Jesus . . . am the root and offspring of David, the bright morning star.'"

ALL ALONG

Barbara Cawthorne Crafton

ONE OF THE LADIES from church stood with me at the sink in the kitchen of the parish house while I cried. When things seemed to be winding down, she had me splash cold water on my face. Then she handed me a clean tea towel with which to dry it: the traditional ending to a good cry. We'd just finished my grandmother's funeral and it had fallen to her to see to me, as there was nobody from my own family to sit with me just now.

You shouldn't cry, she said consolingly, *your grandma is in heaven with Jesus now. You wouldn't want her not to be with Jesus, would you?* Absolutely I would, I thought. But I shook my head no and sniffled a bit. In a few minutes, we went off to deliver me back to my mother.

So much magic left the world when that particular grandmother died. A little more would depart each time someone dear left here for heaven. Love charms us so; it makes us think we are stronger than we really are, when all the while it renders us vulnerable to pain of which we would know nothing were it not for the depth of our love. We think that love conquers all—hah! It is the Trojan horse of sorrow.

I was in no position as a child to criticize the church's doctrine of heaven, insofar as I knew what it was. I also imbibed the popular culture's embroideries on it—angels, for instance, weren't just heavenly messengers of God: some of them were also our dead relatives, newly fitted out with wings. St. Peter was the person you had to see when you arrived, and he kept a ledger in which you'd better hope your name appeared when the time came. The place was more or less like earth, if earth were made of gauzy clouds and golden light, and we would be recognizably ourselves. Except that I would be thinner.

Sometimes the Jehovah's Witnesses came to our door, a girl about my age and her mother, both glumly attired in long skirts and plain blouses. My mother was kind to them, pitying them their dusty trudge around the county every month, and we always bought their pamphlets, *The Watchtower* and *Awake!*—both of which I read with great interest. Their heaven was even more concrete than mine, it seemed: it really was *this very earth* upon which we now stand. Everyone was coming right back here. The pamphlets often showed pictures of what this would be like: happy families strolling in endless fruit orchards, the fathers attentive, the mothers relaxed, the children joyous.

But won't it get too crowded? I asked my mother. She said to just never mind.

The logistical difficulties of the Witnesses' vision of heaven, together with their obvious and intrepid faith in it, started me to wondering. I was getting older now, a teenager, and it no longer seemed wrong to question inherited wisdom. Besides, I was *reading things*—Herman Hesse, Thomas Mann, Victor Frankl. Moliere and Voltaire. None of them seemed the least bit cowed by the demands of religious orthodoxy, and I couldn't help noticing that none of them seemed very interested in heaven. And Dante! It was his hell, of course, that fascinated everybody, not his heaven, but I was struck by how local a place the hereafter was: the civic arguments of fourteenth-century Florence still raged there, and Dante named names. People in the afterlife were still getting what was coming to them in very specific ways. Somehow, it reminded me of the Witnesses.

It would not be long at all before I would jettison the whole idea of heaven altogether. It seemed to me to be the church's sop to simple minds, to pander to the superstitious and the self-absorbed in equal measure: pie-in-the-sky-when-you-die for the suffering, and a halfway decent reason not to bestir oneself overmuch to help them here in earth for everybody else. *I ain't got long to stay here,* said the song. *Oh, okay, so never mind then,* said the church.

I would not shirk my duty to those in need in this callous manner. There was a world in need of transformation, and many of us truly believed we could transform it all by ourselves, and that in short order. The hope of heaven seemed to undercut human ethical responsibility, not to strengthen it. Life's cruelties were simply referred to a higher court—there was no urgent need to solve any of them.

Heaven seemed, also, to abet the lonely self-absorption that was draining the blood out of all of our communal comforts. We traveled in cars, not on trains. We ate in front of the television, and we switched it on as soon as we entered a room. We had private phone lines now, so we never had to wait to make a call. We even *danced* alone, swaying our hips and waving our arms, shifting our weight from foot to foot. We never touched, which meant that all of our touch was quickly distilled down to the sexual, and we found ourselves able to focus on little else. At the same time, our buying power was going through the roof—everything was about consuming. Statistically, shopping became the most popular cultural activity in America. There was nothing you couldn't buy, and nothing you shouldn't own. *You deserve a break today,* McDonald's crooned to us, and who were we to disagree? We could *buy* the fruit of our own deserving, it appeared. A very tangible heaven was come to earth, and it was for sale.

Nothing about this was transcendent of the world of matter, time, space. Nobody would make any money by our turning our thoughts anywhere very numinous, although tidy sums would be made in the angel business in the 1990s: angel books, angel television shows and movies, angel T-shirts, guardian angels you could hang in your car to keep you from crashing, little silver angels you could pin to your lapel to keep you out of trouble. The market domesticated an individualistic spirituality that was ready to be tamed, and it surrendered without a whimper.

Although an aesthetic perspective alone would have condemned the angel boom, its easy venality was what galled me. Where was transformation to take place? Or had we given up on the need for it? A longing for heaven that could look forward to this—

> Behold, I tell you a mystery. We shall not all die, but we shall all be changed, in a moment, in the twinkling of an eye, at the last trumpet. The trumpet shall sound, and the dead shall be raised incorruptible, and we shall be changed. . . .

—enabled the first century to leave the difficult earth behind without a backward glance. And yet Paul, who spoke that hope of heaven to his generation and to ours, occupied himself with successful fundraising for an ambitious program of relief for Judean widows and orphans among new Christians who had no idea where Judea *was*. Almost every letter of Paul's that survives contains a fundraising appeal. His heaven was decidedly otherworldly, but his profound hope in it didn't excuse him from seeing to the needs of the poor. And, unlike the heaven imagined by so many of my contemporaries, his heaven was not conservative. We're not coming back here. We're not going to be just like ourselves, only immortal. *We shall be changed.*

It was in seminary that I began to love Paul, to see beyond what would, in a twentieth-century man, have been homophobia and sexism and was, in his age, just the way things were. He gave me a way to reclaim my hope of heaven without shortchanging a beloved but fallen earth. I was beginning to need the heaven Paul returned to me, too, as the theological and the personal continued to scrape painfully against one another in my life: a stillborn child, the death of my mother, the new and repeated pastoral duty of accompanying people in their last days and of finding words that would be of some use at their funerals. Frequent exposure to death is a fine tutor: one either develops a theology of it or one goes mad with the bitterness of dashed hopes.

I also discovered, as my ordained life unfolded, that a wide and robust interest in ancient Christian forms of devotional life was flourishing beneath the kitsch of pop spirituality. People wanted to learn to pray, to read scripture intelligently and talk about it thoughtfully. People wanted to explore the austere comfort of confession, and to learn about healing prayer. People wanted to read Julian of Norwich, the Desert Fathers and Mothers, St. Francis, Thomas Merton, Anthony Bloom. People read about the Benedictines and visited their monasteries. Labyrinths sprang up in churchyards across the landscape. An album of monastic chant went platinum.

Meanwhile, portions of the new physics were starting to sound awfully familiar. The categories of time and space seemed less discrete now, the linearity of a history that could be expressed in a timeline much less plausible. Past and future occupied a newly imaginable Present that encompassed all things that are and were and ever shall be, in addition, perhaps, to all things that even *could* be. A universe of possibility and simultaneity began to remind of me of heaven, an existence in which nothing is lost.

I began to write about it, to write about stars which we see but which no longer exist. I wrote about moments in history that continue to exist somewhere: perhaps the final notes of the first performance of Handel's *Messiah* still reverberate, however slightly, like the famous flutter of that Chinese butterfly's wings. I wrote about Freud's imagining of the human psyche as an ancient city, level upon level silted up with the sands of time but somehow *alive* in all the levels, with the people still eating and drinking and arguing in them all. I began to think that this was also the way God sees the creation. I began to contemplate the difference between a phenomenon and my *experience* of it: is there a difference? Or is the very fact that a thought is *mine* significant—perhaps the philosophical notion that existence was really a matter of perception had a devotional *use*. Perhaps the external, objective way of thinking about the universe was being found wanting. *Not two,* the Buddhists say. *Not two. One.* If time ceases to be a meaningful category, that terse idea begins to make some sense.

Then it becomes viscerally true that I have done it to Jesus if I have done it to his brother or sister. I am not separate from that sister, that brother: not only have I done it to Jesus, I have done it to myself. I violate myself by violating others. There are no others; there is only *us,* and we are one. That time which is coming is here already, and we are in it now.

Perhaps heaven is an existence in which we see what God sees and love what God loves, in which the seeing and the loving are so potent that they bring forth being, in an eternal time out of time. Perhaps we find our beloved dead there, and understand at once that we have never lost them. Perhaps the kingdom of God is within us, and has been all along.

e.e. cummings, "I carry you in my heart"

FAMOUS LAST WORDS

Peter S. Hawkins

DOES ANYONE EVEN think of heaven apart from the experience of loss? My guess is no. The land of the living is so preoccupying that it takes some radical disenchantment to get most of us to entertain anything beyond the here and now. Or, to put it another way, somebody has to die before the hereafter comes up.

At least that is how heaven entered my little world at the age of three when, without warning, *she* disappeared. One day, the octogenarian lady who bore my father during the reign of Edward VII—who wore hats with plumage and made the sweetest tea—was suddenly no longer at the door of our apartment at midafternoon, ready to pour sugar and play games. Where was she? With my father in England and my mother left to cope alone, the fact of Grandma's death was judged to be too much for me to bear. But something had to be done: I kept asking where she was, kept looking in all the places where she used to go when we played hide and seek. The solution was to take me out on the fire escape at nightfall and have me look at the brightest star in the evening firmament. *That's* where she was now, with God, twinkling down her love for me from her new home in heaven. I no longer had to hunt for her in closets or behind the sofa. Anytime I wanted to visit, all I had to do was wait for evening: She was only a star away.

Inevitably, there comes a time to put away childish things, and Grandma as celestial constellation was certainly one of them. No more twinkling stars. Heaven itself began to seem suspect. Not that I came to disbelieve what the creed speaks of as the "life of the world to come." Who wouldn't want more life or another try at a world, especially if it meant being "embraced by the light," as one heard about from countless near-death experiences? The sure and certain hope of the resurrection that was promised, however, was never spelled out. The souls of the faithful were lost in the abstractions of "joy and felicity," everyone somehow at God's right hand where "there is pleasure for evermore." So the Book of Common Prayer has it when, at the graveside, the priest does his best with what is essentially *carte blanche*— a destination that doesn't seem specific enough to warrant a single Michelin star.

The 1980s and early nineties turned out to be a pro-longed putting away of childish things, a drawn out *memento mori*. The church bells of my parish in New York's West Village tolled for a generation of gay men and provided the rest of us with a lifetime's worth of graveside assurances. AIDS cut through my world like a scythe. Oddly, my faith in the church strengthened even as I wavered in my thinking about Providence. The burial service in particular cast a much-appreciated sober light and, in its lack of sentimentality, made living through those days easier simply by telling truth: "You are dust, and to dust you shall return." "In the midst of life we are in death."

What more could be said? Paul on the resurrection body? Jesus on the many mansions of the Father's house? The psychedelic throne room of Revelation or its cubed jewel box of a city in which every tear is washed away? No. The last thing I wanted was theological discourse or any received attempt at the picture perfect. Perhaps I was overtaken by a cranky refusal to be comforted; in any event, most of the efforts to do so—and in this regard "sympathy" cards are the worst offenders—seemed cheap and offensive.

Then there was *Long Time Companion,* the 1990 film that coincided with the death of my thirty-five-year-old partner, Luis Varela. I felt as if I had been given a gift when the funeral in the movie turned out to have been shot in my New York parish, in the same sanctuary where Luis had been welcomed (on the basis of my faith, not his own) as a lamb of God's flock. "Receive him into the arms of your mercy," the priest had said, "into the blessed rest of everlasting peace, and into the glorious company of the saints in light." But as opposed to everyone around me in the theater, I rejected the vision of a Fire Island reunion of the living and the dead that brought the film to its conclusion. Talk about childish things! Yet there was not a dry eye in the house except for my own. Let's face it, I felt like saying (but wisely did not), our beloveds are *not* going to rise from the dunes and, looking fabulous, rush into our open arms at water's edge. I could not bear the "all manner of thing shall be well" of it all. Hadn't everything irrevocably changed? To resist the fact that it had, that the dead as we knew them in all the old familiar places were gone, was just fantasy. I wanted nothing to do with it.

And then, as part of the long dirge of that period, my father died after a long bout with Parkinson's, and at the untragic age of eighty-one. By this point my parents had relocated from New York to New England; the family had also dwindled to a handful of people I hardly knew. No one had gotten around to organizing a proper funeral, and yet I felt out of some very primitive sense of what the dead are owed that something needed to be done. I asked the parish priest of a church in New Haven if the next Saturday 9 A.M. Eucharist might be offered in memory of my father. I was not Prince Hamlet with a paternal ghost to assuage, but somehow it seemed important to lay Dad to rest, perhaps especially since I felt that I had failed him in his last years (or maybe all the years that preceded them). Ours was not a father–son relationship "made in heaven."

The priest was happy to oblige me, and so, with the very odd assortment of people who go to an Episcopal church on a Saturday morning, we prayed for the repose of Thomas William Hawkins. During the service my mind wandered, as it inevitably does in church, but this time into a state that, were I living in another age, might have been called a vision. ("Daydream" I'll call it now.) I imagined my father in a casino, gleefully wasting money with a zest I had never once seen in him. A depressed survivor of the Depression, he had always been pathologically careful *not* to spend. Money was to be held on to, saved for a rainy day or perhaps simply to be saved. It was never wasted. But there he was, in the lurid light of a gambling hall—quarters flying, one-armed bandits pumping away—as if there were no tomorrow. He was a very happy man.

When I came to my senses afterward, I wondered if I had seen Dad in purgatory, learning to let go and have fun, no longer burdened by the need to save but free at last to be crazy and irresponsible. At first, playing the slot machines would be torture, because wasting money was, so to speak, against his religion. But maybe this is what happens when you die: the arms of mercy that receive you set you loose in a place where you would not otherwise be caught dead. They bid you do the opposite of what you'd done in life— nudge you to go to the *other* side of the territory you had come to know, during your eighty-something years, like the back of your hand. Rather than being as comfortable as an old shoe, as satisfying as a long-held dream come true, maybe the afterlife came as a shock. After all, didn't Jesus say at the very end of the Revelation to John, "Behold, I make all things new"?

Nothing in my own religious upbringing led me to imagine my father in purgatory. Rather, a childhood spent

in the company of Roman Catholics had put it on my religious radar screen. I was both fascinated and repelled by the
little placards in St. Patrick's Cathedral that promised days
off in exchange for prayers said. Like first communion suits
and statues that wept or bled, purgatory was for my Catholic
friends, not for me. It took Dante to open up the "middle
kingdom" between a hell I (nervously) didn't believe in and
a heaven I couldn't imagine. His *Purgatorio* made deep sense:
The souls who painstakingly make their way up the
Mountain are constantly in process, moving from one state
to another. As they move they also make progress, letting go
of everything in mortal life that weighed them down or
blinded them to light. Something positive is also taking
place: where once vice held the penitent in its grip, the cor-
responding virtue begins to gain the upper hand.

I love in particular what Dante does on the Terrace of
Pride. It's there that the souls of the proud are bent under
the more or less massive stones they carry on their backs,
each of which represents the false *persona* that spiritually
crippled and deformed them in life—what Iris Murdoch
called the "fat, relentless ego." The soul bends under its own
weight until it decides to let go of its burden; it is a decision
that can take centuries in the afterlife to achieve. At that
point, and with the freedom that comes with humility, it at
last stands tall, able to move on to the next of the seven terraces (one for each of the deadly sins) and ready for the next
stage. My father's tendency to hoard could be cured, in
other words, by an exercise in prodigality. Let the quarters
fly!

Dante's notion of purgatory bears no resemblance to the
temporary hell or "prison house" (to recall the ghost of
Hamlet's father) that Catholic tradition otherwise imagined.
Rather, it's a hospital for the healing of brokenness; a school
for the learning of truth; an incubator in which caterpillars
grow up to be butterflies; a conservatory where soloists
become a chorus and speakers develop a use for "we" and

"us" in addition to "I," "me," and "mine." Life sentences are
not served; rather, lives are rewritten.

Two other analogies, both of them anachronistic, also
spring to mind. Purgatory is an Ellis Island in the old days,
a naturalization center where new arrivals from our earthly
cities become citizens of the City of God. Or the whole
experience of the Mountain can be likened to psychoanaly-
sis, where the analysand painfully unties the knots of the past
so as to live more freely in an unencumbered future. Dante's
hell is all about repetition-compulsion, an endless replay of
the sinner's "song of myself." Purgatory, on the contrary, is
dynamic, dedicated to change and transformation. Its end is
the rebirth of a self that is free to be interested in other souls
and other things.

But what about heaven? Here Dante is less useful, or at
least less congenial to an early twenty-first-century
American who cherishes the idea of progress and self-
improvement, the notion that there is always more to do and
a better place to go. Imagine the disappointment, then,
when the pilgrim's journey to God reaches its destination in
the Empyrean and heaven turns out to be a white rose
(which is also, somehow, a coliseum!) and the pilgrim dis-
covers that every one of the blessed, like children in a
schoolroom, has an assigned seat. Could the vision of God,
the "joy and felicity" promised in the burial service, really
amount to a corporate viewing of the Trinity—forever?

Thomas Aquinas thought so. Because heaven was perfect
it was absolutely static, with the blessed enjoying a beatific
immobility. Despite the crowd scene around the divine
throne in Revelation, Thomas did not believe it necessary
that there should be a cloud of witnesses sharing in the
divine contemplation: "If there were but one soul enjoying
God, it would be [perfectly] happy, though having no neighbor to love" (*Summa Theologiae* I, II, q. 4, art. 8, reply obj. 3).
Here Thomas differed from Augustine, who said that one of
the ways that the blessed might see God "face to face"

would be to perceive him in the glorified faces of one another (*City of God* 22.29). If you seek the Lord, in other words, just look around you.

Dante humanizes his heaven as well, by having the blessed anticipate their resurrection bodies not only because they long to be whole again themselves but also to be "in touch" with their mothers, fathers, and loved ones (*Paradiso* 14.65). Likewise, within the arena of the white rose, where the whole company of heaven is centered on the Trinity's Eternal Light, they also beam their love toward the Virgin Mary. Indeed, her mother, St. Anne, simply cannot take her eyes off her adored daughter even while singing her Hosannas to Father, Son, and Holy Spirit (*Paradiso* 32.132–135). *Paradiso* includes an afterlife for special affections, as St. Anne's love for Mary and Dante's enduring bond with Beatrice make clear. The notion of ongoing relationships has since become commonplace: almost everyone who believes in heaven imagines that those we love best in this life will be those we love in eternity. "Blessed be the tie that binds" has become received wisdom for most Christians and a cornerstone of faith for Latter Day Saints.

Yet even the most fervent aficionado of the *Commedia* must admit that finally, "When the trumpet of the Lord shall sound, and time shall be no more," as the gospel hymn would have it, Dante's blessed are going to be sitting still, looking up to the divine light, and focusing (world without end) on God. Hmmm. On the one hand, what more could a creature desire than to be in a perpetual state of wonder— to be lost in the pages of a spellbinding book that need never come to an end, or singing a Hallelujah Chorus that does not have to resolve into a final Amen? On the other hand, the prospect of endlessly sitting still and paying attention, no matter how you package it, threatens to seem more like high school detention than bliss. Or worse yet, it reminds one of the ranks of Mother Angelica's robotic nuns on cable television who, with eyes averted from the camera's gaze, tell their beads in scarily perfect synchrony. The truth is that the vast majority of us suffer from an inability to pay attention to anything for very long. We would have to be changed, and changed utterly, for any such eternal prospect to please us, let alone be the divine kingdom we pray to come every time we say the Lord's Prayer.

But perhaps *that* is the point about the world to come: the only way it can be imagined honestly is as utterly different from what we already know, *not* a continuation of what gives us pleasure right now. Still, in the interim, what's a twenty-first-century Christian to hope for, knowing that all bets are off when it comes to the Real Thing?

Since turning sixty, and despite vigorous good health, I find myself thinking about final moments and last words. How will I face it and what will I say? The deathbed should be the moment of truth, even when one is "making believe" ahead of time. How, then, do I imagine what's next, and what have I actually taken away from a Master of Divinity, over thirty years of Dante study, and even more decades spent marinating in tradition?

If ever there were an occasion to contemplate a single possibility, the deathbed would be it. And yet, at least right now, I am of two minds: I have (in the language of computers) a split screen. Because of the religious worlds I've traveled in, I foresee angels, archangels, and all the company of heaven. Here are the saints in light, including (who knows?) a Grandma, a mother, a father, and a Luis. There are flashes of lightning and peals of thunder. Ten thousand times ten thousand gather before the divine throne. I think of the most solemn of Baroque high masses, with clouds of incense and all my favorite music.

But because I am a child of our age, with a deep suspicion of fantasy's smokescreen, the other portion of my afterlife screen is a complete blank. Whether all black or all white doesn't matter: There is absolutely nothing to behold. Lights out. It is finished.

All or Nothing? Right now it is a toss, but at my end I am sure to make some version of Pascal's wager. In this essay, moreover, I want to go for broke and opt for a single scenario. It won't be some amalgam of John's Revelation and Dante's *Paradiso;* nor will it be "nothing." I'll refrain from anticipating anything that can be seen whatsoever, except with what scripture speaks of as the "eyes of the heart." Instead, I'll put my life and my death into a single spoken line, which will be as close as I can come now to preparing for the great adventure.

If my deathbed permits the silly as well as the sincere, I'll recall Diaghilev's charge to his star dancer, Nijinsky— *"Etonnez-moi"*—and say to the Almighty, "Astonish me, O Lord, and let it be world without end, Amen." That is, in fact, what I mean: God, bring on the divine "whatever"! As the collect reminds us, you are wont to bestow more than we desire or deserve, so take me—I'm yours.

But more likely, not wanting to push it, I'll play it straight. In such a moment as my play's last scene I will not presume to be original, interesting, or anything other than soberly true. I'll pluck from memory a line from the New Testament that was taken from the Psalms. I will let my last word be the one that I hope I can express with my final breath, the one that Luke reports that Jesus spoke from the cross, and that sums up absolutely everything that needs saying: "Father, into your hands I commend my spirit." The rest, whatever it may be, is simply not up to me.

BAMBOO HEAVEN

Amy Blackmarr

Heaven:...a spiritual state of everlasting communion
with God; a place or condition of utmost happiness; the
dwelling place of God.
                    —*Webster's Seventh New Collegiate Dictionary*

WHEN I WAS ELEVEN, I often spent my afternoons in
a tiny clearing inside the bamboo that bordered Miss Ibba's
yard. I found the place by chance one early South Georgia
summer night during kick-the-can with the neighborhood
kids, and while the others climbed trees or hid out behind
the azaleas or under the wheelbarrow Clarence had left
behind from his pruning, I sat in the muffled silence with
the utter certainty that none of those kids would find me.
Hidden behind a screen of reeds, I could easily have been
discovered, had they known where to look. They didn't
know. They saw only the bamboo.

As the summer passed, I found trails that led away from
my clearing and meandered deeper into the reeds, some
dividing into branches that headed off in many directions,
others simply ending. I thought fairies or elves must live in
the bamboo and hide when they saw me coming. I left them
presents of pink camellias from the neighbors' bushes, and
little sprays of mimosa blossoms and crape myrtle.

Sometimes I took my dog Pepper into the bamboo with me, and a book, and there, safe and undisturbed and at peace with all the worldly wisdom my eleven years had brought me, I spent long moments in perfect harmony with leafy bamboo and dog and damp earth and book and the close South Georgia summer air. Heaven lay about me in those moments, and it nurtured the heaven I held within.

Now I am forty-eight and feel no longer wise and rarely heavenly. I am not often enough prayerful and too often not at peace with my own long tangle of years, much less with the wider world in all its suffering. Everything seems chaotic and restless, and I feel at a loss for how to settle it down. People are bursting into flame. Violence is ubiquitous. The sweetness and light I envisioned in my twenties really does seem like a Victorian ideal. And I have chores to do, divine chores, and I'm falling behind.

But I mustn't make too much of that—the falling behind. Instead, as one does, I keep going. I try to make the best of things, and make what small good changes I can. And sometimes into the center of all my Faustian struggles comes what my poetry professor used to call a "teaching moment," only the teacher is . . . well, it's God.

Our house is two rooms and a hallway. Squeezed together in our house are a kitchen, a laundry, a bed, two computers, three guitars and a violin, some other musical instruments, a large dog, many books, and two toilets just big enough to sit down on. When company comes to see us, my husband, Chase, tells them we live in the command center and that our mansion is in a parallel universe and then he invites the company back outside, onto the patio, which is nearly the same size as the house. The patio is a sanctuary now, but it wasn't always.

When we arrived at our rented South Georgia bungalow on the threshold of a hundred-degree summer, the patio was a hundred and fifty square feet of glaring white concrete that gave off heat devils in the middle of the day. Nothing about it was restful or sane and so I, having just come from five years in the mossy peace-laden woods of the Blue Ridge mountains, headed straight for the local nursery and loaded up my car with plants. I had to tamp down all that antiseptic garishness with something soft and green. Having no room to create a garden indoors, I resolved to create one without.

So I bought trees. I bought flowers. I bought palms and ferns and ivies, hibiscus and azaleas and gardenias, willows and bamboo and tea olives and hollies—dozens of living, waving, water-lush plants, some of them blooming and all in profusion and all of them in pots. Over a six-month summer in sweltering heat, I lined the inside of the patio with plants and then covered the ledges and surrounded the whole space with trees in every imaginable shade of green. I arranged the bamboo at one end, where I could hear it rustling, and set the willows on either side of the low front steps so that every time I walked between them, their long limbs brushed the top of my head. It felt, Chase said, as though his soul were being washed clean every time he came into the house. Those willows gave him back his balance, he said.

And now, after a year, my patio garden has established its own ecological balance. I've spied lizards and green anoles running willy-nilly along the ledges. Bees in the lantana. Ladybugs on the crape myrtles, eating the aphids. A mourning dove has taken up residence nearby, and Saturday morning, while I was sitting under the patio umbrella at an old wrought-iron table among the ferns, drinking my coffee, a nuthatch came to sit in the holly. Chase and I still have to step over each other indoors, but outside is a spacious, scent-filled, green growing garden, a kind of grown-up, cultivated version of the bamboo haven I took refuge in as a child.

It seems no great wonder, then, that when I enter this scented cloister with book and coffee, my calamities vanish. Knots come untangled. I become that mild, untroubled child again, for in the outer quiet, all my inner crashing around settles down, and there for a while I remember that deep down in the center of my soul I am in love with God, and I can come back into the wider world and resume my chores. The heaven without brings peace within, and my peace-filled, God-renewed spirit can travel back out into the world again.

Sometimes when I'm in a cantankerous mood I rearrange things. It calms me. Ordinarily I'd rearrange the furniture, but there's not enough room. So I move all the pots around the patio, into the corners, along the ledges. I work at this for hours, like a *feng shui* master, getting the placement just right.

I also move the patio saint around, into the ivy or onto the steps, from one end of the garden to the other, and at his feet at various times I've placed ceramic rabbits, wandering Jew, a basket of seashells, and pots of lavender. I've hung a blue crystal on the wall behind him and blue daze above his head. He is St. Fiacre, the patron saint of gardeners, whose spade had only to touch the earth to bring life springing up out of the ground. He's a seventh-century saint reduced to concrete, but he's still performing miracles.

What happened was, last Sunday afternoon, in a fit of creative (cantankerous) energy, I moved St. Fiacre from among the columbine, where he had stood since last winter, into a miniature shrine I built for him beside the front door. He would be, I thought, a kind of garden door guardian to send us off every morning with a blessing and welcome us home at the end of the day. I surrounded him with fountain grass and white verbena, marigolds and lilies and caches of stones I've found in fields over the years. All that was missing, I thought when I finally got him situated, was the sound of water. If I only had a fountain...but never mind. It was enough.

Evening drew down. Chase and I ate our supper and sat down to watch a movie. Then rain came. A storm blew in. The wind picked up, and in minutes, the rain was horizontal. Water poured over the eaves, and the old pines I could see from the window were bending dangerously sideways.

Suddenly we heard a crash and a series of thumps and other noises, and the dog smashed himself against my chair, and I realized that something violent had happened on the patio. All of my lovingly tended, fussed-over plants had surely toppled off the ledges, blown across the driveway, their pots shattered; the willows and bamboo were surely in ruins, the hollies and crape myrtles demolished...for in the wake of such a wind, chaos had certainly ensued.

"I can't look!" I said when the storm abated and Chase opened the patio door. I refused to budge out of my chair. "Don't tell me."

Chase stood in the doorway, looking out, silent.

Seconds passed. Chase sighed.

"What?" I said.

"You've got to see this." He flipped on the porch lights.

"I don't want to." I put my hands over my face and peered out through my fingers. "Just tell me."

"Come look."

I got up and went to stand beside Chase, my heart a rock. The patio umbrella, which had been open and is huge and heavy, had been lifted clear out of its socket and blown down onto the patio.

I shook my head, imagining catastrophe. Dozens of potted plants and trees and barely room to walk among them without knocking them over and a leviathan suddenly takes wing and crash-lands in the middle of them all. I couldn't stand to think of it, all that *damage*. My sacramental space ruined, my garden communion broken! How long would it take me to build it all back again?

Chase put his hand on my shoulder and I steeled myself, took a breath, and looked around, wondering what could be saved, what I could replace . . . and what I saw staggered me. Except for a single upended pot of purslane and a crack in a blue ceramic pot I'd never much liked anyway, *there wasn't any damage at all*. A Boston fern, quadrupled in size since last spring, had cushioned the leviathan's fall. Somehow it had simply closed its wings and landed at the feet of St. Fiacre, who stood in his shrine unfazed, his garden spade raised as if in benediction.

"Impossible," I said.

"Still," said Chase. "There it is."

I lingered in the door a while beside the saint with his spade, marveling at the calm, listening to the bamboo rustle in the breeze, breathing in that fragrance of wet earth and pine that comes after a rain, until I realized that by sheer force of habit I was holding a pen.

Now every day I've been going to work, where I catalog books at the local library. And when I come home in the late afternoon I take care to spend an hour or so on the patio, where I water and fertilize and rearrange, worry and fuss and attend, cultivating heaven in every quiet breath I breathe and every peace-laden thought I think. I tend all these shrines—the green, growing garden without, the sacred heart within—because I am the patron saint of peace. I am the small guardian of the world. In the ordinary miracle of my own life I make God's home at the center of my being, nurture God's peace in all my relations, and build a heaven in this wide, great garden of a world.

ON CELESTIAL MUSIC
Rick Moody

1. Heaven and Premium Stereo Equipment
Music is of God, and music is with God, and music is how
God expresses him- or herself, and music is everywhere, and
music is a crafty art and is completed in places inside us, in
the impossible-to-locate precincts wherein there is access to
feelings that we might otherwise ignore. Or: the abstraction
of music is how God conceals his or her complicated plan.
Or: the abstraction of music, its connection to deep feeling,
has all the traces of the Holy Ghost, so it seems to me, and
if I didn't understand this logically as a kid, I at least understood how moving music was, when I was first going to
church in the suburbs.

Back then, I wanted to lay eyes on things. Because when
you're a kid you're open to all kinds of things, but you trust
what's in front of your face. I remember feeling that the
praying part of the religious service was deeply suspect.
People would get this expression on their faces, something
near to earnest self-regard. I was supposed to overlook this
earnest mien, and I was meant to know intuitively the pre-
cise organization of hands for prayer, and then I was supposed to know what to murmur and to whom. And then
there was the posturing *after* church. Forget about it! That
was not what I associated with God, heaven, the sublime, the

celestial. There was some talk, during Sunday school, about heaven, and it was always of the old-guy-with-a-beard variety, and I never believed any of that. I had a bullshit detector where ideology was concerned. I resisted what I was told, even if it was good for me, even if it made the world a better place.

What moved me was the music. Music filled me with this intense feeling about the state of things, from my earliest recollections. Not only the organ music before and after services. The organ music was sublime, even when I didn't know anything about harmony and counterpoint. Organ music scared me and demanded something of me, by virtue of its grandiosity. (This would perhaps be the moment to say the obvious, that if earthly music is played in heaven, then J. S. Bach really must be the *cappellmeister*.) There was also the choir singing during church service. My mom was known to sing in the choir (later on I did a bit of it myself), and there was a lot of singing going on around my house generally. The human voice, raised in song, was important, was unearthly, gave access to the numinous. And obviously there are indications of this across the centuries of recorded time, almost wherever you look. In David's psalms, for example: "O sing to the Lord a new song; sing his praise in the congregation of the faithful."[1] I wouldn't have had any idea what this meant, back when I was first in church. But I knew I liked the singing.

At about the same time, my mother became highly partisan about the popular recording artists known as Simon and Garfunkel. We had a lot of their LPs. In fact, we had all of them. I could make a good argument about the sublime and the song known as "The Sound of Silence," which would then lead to a discussion of John Cage and the theological importance of silence, but I'm putting that off for

---

1. And especially in Psalms 146 to 150, "Praise him with the blast of the trumpet; praise him with the harp and lyre. Praise him with timbrel and dances; praise him upon the strings and pipe. Praise him with ringing cymbals; praise him upon the clashing cymbals. Let everything that has breath praise the Lord. Alleluia."

another time. Instead, I want to talk about a mostly forgotten Simon and Garfunkel tune on the album *Wednesday
Morning, 3 A.M.*, entitled "Sparrow." This song, in the folk
genre that characterized early Simon and Garfunkel recordings, unfolds as a series of sympathetic questions about a
sparrow, addressed to the other preoccupied living things of
the world: Who will love a little sparrow? Who will speak to
it a kindly word? A swan is posed this question, a field of
wheat, an oak tree, and yet all of these eminences decline the
opportunity to become stewards of the common sparrow,
himself adrift on the callousness of the world, where it is the
fate of tenderness to be crushed. Then in the last verse the
earth steps in, having been asked the same question. The
earth responds with a forceful affirmative, in regards to the
sparrow, quoting from scripture, "From dust were ye made
and dust ye shall be."

     This little song shook my earthly foundations back in
Connecticut, where my early music appreciation lessons
were taking place. Not only because it had that mysterious,
unearthly quality that English folk music had about it. Not
only because of the harmonies, which were always pretty
extraordinary in the Simon and Garfunkel corpus. Above all,
the song moved me because it depicted so much loss and so
much weariness, and because the sparrow, it seemed to me,
had to die. These days, "Sparrow" might sound a bit quaint to
the average listener, owing to its self-evident allegorical scaf-
folding. But this is also what makes folk songs profound, that
they are simple, unadorned, and eager to confront religious,
philosophical, and political questions. They are modal, poly-
semous, difficult to pin down; they are fairy tales with
melodies. This makes folk music ideal for a kid who's six or
seven. I didn't have any defense against the emotional freight
of the song, and it devastated me. What was "Sparrow" about
for me? "Sparrow" was about loving the forgotten, the mar-
ginalized, the sick, homely, and despised. It was about how
everything has to die, and if heaven is a locale wherein the

injustice of earthly mortality is repaired, uh, for *eternity,* then "Sparrow," in its radical acceptance of the spurned little bird, points in the direction of heavenly music, what it might do, how it might make the case for paradise.

I guess I'm covering up if I'm not saying that I admired this particular song at a troubling time, the time when my own parents were divorcing. I suppose it's obvious that I was identifying with the sparrow, feeling, like him, as though refuge from heartache was hard to come by. In this way, many of the songs I liked then seem kind of sad. For example: another song I cherished was "Golden Slumbers" by the Beatles. It's the lullaby on a very complex, protean album, *Abbey Road.* Let me explain where I listened to it. My parents had this new stereo system, in a big wooden cabinet in the living room. It was a *hi-fi,* in the classic sense of the term, and it was maybe the expensive hi-fi that they bought to convince themselves, through amplification, that they were more allied and resilient than they were. My father, who never seemed to be home, was not there while we were making dinner, and so he probably wouldn't remember my mother putting on *Abbey Road,* whereupon we would dance around to the rock numbers, like "Mean Mr. Mustard" and "Come Together." Nor was he there when we sang along with "Golden Slumbers" and "Here Comes the Sun."

Eventually, an evening came to pass that I understood as the moment during which my parents were discussing how to tell us they were separating. They were enclosed in that family room with the expensive hi-fi. The louvered drawing room doors were closed. There was an unsettling silence in the house. We (my sister, brother, and I) looked at these closed doors from up the staircase, between the dowels supporting the banister. Something lasting and sad was taking place. It was obvious. And soon my mother came to break the news to us. Ever after, when I've imagined this scene, I've heard in my head, chief among other songs, "Golden

Slumbers." Once, as the song suggests, there *was* a way to get back home. In the past tense. The song still calls forth that loss in me, that time after certainty. Does this melancholy reside in the lyrics, because the relationship between the singer of the song (Paul McCartney) and the children to whom he sings, is, arguably, not dissimilar to the relationship between the divine (from a perch in heaven) and the beloved flock here on earth?

Actually, I probably liked "Golden Slumbers" because no one sang me lullabies as a kid. I had no idea about *agape* and *caritas.* I had no idea about heaven. I was skeptical. Even a lullaby, from my point of view, would have been like a happy ending in a movie. Happy endings were for people who believed any nonsense that came along. So I liked "Golden Slumbers" because I secretly wanted somebody to sing a lullaby to me. Admitting such a thing makes me uncomfortable. And yet it was from unfulfilled longing that I formulated some ideas of that *elsewhere* of paradise, the place where no longing goes unfulfilled.

2. The Heavenly Jukebox
So far it sounds like I'm making a playlist for a heavenly jukebox. What would be the selections on such a jukebox? Is this jukebox any good? From an earthly point of view, I imagine that if there is music in heaven, it should celebrate virtues and ideals. Does the heavenly jukebox therefore contain only songs by Pat Boone or Deborah Gibson? Does God—whatever he, she, it is—have some amazing celestial version of iTunes, where you can hear the songs you like all day long as long as you have, as a virtuous individual, gained admission to the celestial realms? Could I, for example, hear "The Spirit of Radio" by Rush in heaven (assuming I'm virtuous), even though I won't allow myself to listen to it on earth because it is simply too embarrassing? What if hearing

Rush would (arguably) make me happy for all eternity? Do people in this kingdom of the worthy get to play Whitesnake around the clock, just because they are good and deserving? Or have they transcended Whitesnake, having passed beyond the earthly realms? Do they allow Metallica in heaven? What about that Finnish band where the lead singer wears Satanic horns? Maybe he's a really good hardworking guy, despite wearing the horns, and is just trying to provide for his Finnish wife and child? Will he be admitted into heaven and be able there to play a big gig with Jimi Hendrix sitting in?

Does God allow celestial broadcasts of Led Zeppelin's "Stairway to Heaven"? Or "Heaven Is A Place On Earth" by Belinda Carlisle? Or "Just Like Heaven" by the Cure? Or "Heaven" by the Talking Heads, or "Pennies From Heaven"? Or the oft-covered "Knockin' On Heaven's Door," which seems to imply that the doorway to heaven is constructed of such a lightweight material that you *could* knock on it. These songs all have *heaven* in the title, but I don't think they are all good songs, except maybe the Dylan composition, and they don't teach me anything about what kind of music exists in heaven.

And what kind of musical instruments *do* they have in heaven? In the old days, they had trumpets and lutes. Many accounts substantiate this point. Are we to believe that heavenly instrumental groups stopped innovating a thousand years ago? Unlikely! So are there, in fact, electric guitars in heaven, or things that sound like electric guitars? What about synthesizers or digital samplers? Do they have the latest plug-ins for computer-based music in heaven? Do you have to clear your samples in heaven (because stealing is a venal sin), or can you go ahead and pilfer copyrighted music to your heart's content? What about all those exotic instruments? Tibetan bowls? Mouth harps? Are there didjeridoos in heaven? Are these instruments available to all who need them for the sake of expression?

Well, it's a real stretch to posit a jukebox in heaven, and
I don't think God is a jukebox, and you cannot take your
iPod with you when you are gone, and there is no digital
sampler and no mixing board to connect it to. Music in
heaven probably would not have lightweight lyrics, or even
unimpeachably useful lyrics like "All You Need Is Love," and
since it's unlikely that we will reach heaven in our corporeal
forms, we may not have ears with which to listen to music,
nor voices with which to sing it.

3. The Groove in Heaven
Common time is said to be the time signature that closely
resembles the human heartbeat, and 4/4 is also the time signature with the best opportunity for the *groove*. If in my
early life I might perhaps have advanced the notion that the
music in heaven would be noteworthy for lyrical exegesis
on subjects like compassion and love, in my teens I would
have thought it was all about the groove. Bass and drums,
those were the things that made music heavenly, as when
you are a teenager or a young adult and you like the endless
groove, for example, in "Sister Ray" by the Velvet
Underground, and you are willing to hear that groove go
around and around, and you do not exactly care what the
lyrics say, if indeed you are able to decipher them. The view
from rock club floors and dance clubs and mosh pits is that
music is ecstatic, that the groove is ecstatic, and if music is
ecstatic then heavenly music should be the acme of this
ecstasy. It should be all about union and the sense of community, things that are self-evident at concerts and clubs.

When I am in the groove, the groove is good. Thus, the
teenage version of myself imagined that heaven, or paradise,
was where there was always a good groove, and all kinds of
people could dance around to it together, for light years at a
time. When I was in the groove, wallowing in the one-four

chord progression, let's say, or during a song by Funkadelic, then it was all about how many people you could get playing at one time, and the entire audience was on its feet and chanting along with some line like "Get up on the downstroke! Everybody get up!" even if many listeners were not exactly sure what the downstroke was nor why they should get up on it. At one time, I would have said that if heaven could not deliver on these things, on the promise of community and on a music that has a good groove to it, then I didn't think heaven was heavenly.

Meanwhile, it would be logical and easy to make the argument that the groove has a sexual cast about it, and that people respond to the groove because it is suggestive of the pace and rhythm of sexuality. If this were the case, then again we might have to disqualify this music from heaven, on the basis that there is no corporeal resurrection, in my view, and thus no need for music that appeals to the carnal (or procreative) ecstasy of the flesh. Perhaps for similar reasons, Cotton Mather frowned upon dancing: "Their Children dance, and They go down the Grave into Hell."

In the vicinity of this notion of the sexual cast of the groove for me would be the related notion of intoxication in heaven generally. There is no need for intoxication in heaven. I suppose this is kind of obvious. Why would you need to be intoxicated there? Up there, you have not fallen short, you are not in a condition of wanting, you are theoretically happy, and so you are not looking for the music or drugs or spirits to intoxicate you in any way. You don't need to be bludgeoned by the music in heaven, you don't need to dance until you are exhausted, you don't need one more rousing chorus, because you don't need to be roused, and you are not going to get banged up in the mosh pit, nor are you going to suffer hearing loss, and no one is going to cough during the most beautiful part of the aria, and no one is going to climb over you to get to their seat during the opening measures of the second movement of the symphony.

4. Music for Canyons

I bring up this fact of intoxication because of how quitting drinking improved and defined my own spiritual life. I did not have any genuine conviction about heaven, or God, or spirituality, or an afterlife, or anything else, really, between the ages of fifteen and twenty-six, when I was often busy doing other things, most of them not very good for me. This came to an end in 1987,[2] after which it occurred to me to go back to church, out of gratitude for my reprieve, and for the remission of the considerable pain I'd been living with.

Music also came back into my life in a number of ways. First, I started dabbling in it again. I'd taught myself guitar as a teenager, and so I bought a guitar anew and began practicing it, and I began writing songs, which I had also done when young. I also started listening to things in a new way. I can chart the subsequent metamorphosis in my musical taste with a number of recordings I first heard on a local new music program that was broadcast each night in New York City.

First among the discoveries of that time was the music of Arvo Pärt. While I can't remember exactly which piece I first heard by Pärt, I can remember the first album I bought, which was the ECM release called *Tabula Rasa*. On this recording, both the piece called "Cantus in Memory of Benjamin Britten" and the orchestral piece "Fratres" genuinely moved me in ways that "serious" music rarely had. These pieces, which are said to have been composed as a way out of the dead end of serial music and academic atonality, are frankly spiritual and completely tonal, using elements of early music, like plainsong, for their raw material. Elsewhere, Pärt set liturgical texts. For these reasons, and because the pieces are *so* simple, there is some grumbling in

2. Committed to psychiatric hospital, got sober, etc.

classical music circles about Pärt's work. He's not serious, he's conservative, etc.

I didn't care about any of this when I first heard these recordings, and I still don't. Pärt's compositions split me open like I was an oyster, and the way they did it was by exploiting the simple harmonies of ancient Western music, the kind of dignity and stateliness that I associated with the music of the church as I first heard it. In a way, I can't explain what it is about this simplicity and tonality that was so moving to me. And I'm not sure I want to. *Tintinnabuli* is the term that Pärt has in the past used to describe these pieces, meaning that they sound like bells or have the unadorned grace of bells.

Pärt led me to other things. Not just to spiritually inclined classical music, but to kinds of music that were organized along similar principles, where there was simplicity and elemental harmonics, and where the devotion was to serenity and austerity and to the notion of music itself. That is, I wasn't as interested in the noise that was very moving to me as a young person, nor was I interested in virtuosity for its own sake. Rather, I was after a rather baroque idea that tonality *was* spiritual, and even divine. I was therefore moved by minimalism, by LaMonte Young, by Meredith Monk, by chamber music like the Penguin Café Orchestra, by early music, by Hildegard von Bingen, William Byrd, Purcell. It also seemed as if anything contemporary that I liked had a lot of echo in it, as if music that was made in canyons was somehow better than music that was made anywhere else. Music that celebrated or was illustrative of sound and nature, and the physicality of things.[3] Maybe in this way I'm beginning to answer the question *why music in heaven at all?* One thing that everybody always talks about in heaven is the *light*. Dante talks a lot about the light in *Paradiso*. Such a pleasing light! When other chroniclers have made it up there

3. I am not, however, a partisan of the music known as *New Age*. I do not endorse bland sheets of wallpaper over a machined bed of "exotic" percussion, even if I am in a spa or a yoga studio.

and reported back, there's always ecstatic light in their description. No paintings, no sculptures, no epic poems. No one in heaven is busy making installations or performing performance art. But there *is* music.

This goes all the way back, I imagine, to when there was music to the planets themselves, the heavenly bodies. It's an old perception, the music of the spheres. You find it as far back as Cicero (in *De Republica*), and if he was writing it down, he probably wasn't the first to have remarked on the subject: "This music is produced by the impulse and the motion of these spheres themselves. The unequal intervals between them are arranged according to a strict proportion, and so the high notes blend agreeably with the low, and thus various sweet harmonies are produced." Music, according to this view, is an essential quality of creation, and we might mention especially the sublimity of harmony. And, as Cicero further observes, along with the ubiquity of heavenly music goes the tendency of men to want to imitate it: "Skillful men reproducing this celestial music on stringed instruments have thus opened the way for their own return to this heavenly region, as other men of outstanding genius have done by spending their lives on Earth in the study of things divine."

Why music then? Because when we sing it and play it, we are not only imitating the things that are, but we are praising them, praising the things that are, and praising is good, and you find it, too, in almost any account of heaven. The angels sing their praises, and when we sing, according to, among others, the Levites, we are imitating the angels.

5. Heaven and Non-Being
Still, in the end, any discussion of heaven hinges on the injustice of non-being, and whether you are worried about this injustice. This seems to me the weakest link in the argu-

ment about heaven. That there must be some reward for living through this life in the first world? Living through the
war and greed and hypocrisy and selfishness? Maybe there *is*
no reward, really, but having done a good job here! That is
its own reward! The reward for living in a dignified way in
the first world is dignified life in and of itself. Who isn't full
of longing for a place better than this place? Who, driving
through Elizabeth, New Jersey, or Omaha, Nebraska, or
Indianapolis, Indiana, wouldn't long for an idealized heaven?
And if the longing is good and human, what need for
heaven? Longing and compassion and tenderness *are* heavenly, and they make you better than you otherwise were.

If the whole belief in heaven depends on a fear of non-
being, then it's no more realistic than the notion of naked
people sitting around on clouds playing lutes. Myself, I have
no fear of non-being. I fear mortal pain, which so often
seems to precede non-being, but otherwise I don't fear the
end of the author of these particular sentences, and I don't
need, for his sake, everlasting life. There's enough hassle
involved with the temporary life. Everlasting life would be
closer to hell, for me, than any fiery lake clogged with politicians. Because what would one *do* with eternity?

Unless, for the sake of argument, we are simply talking
about energy. Unless we are talking about the little spark
calved off the big creative first cause. Maybe we are simply
talking about our ability to unite with that first cause.
Maybe we are talking about a union that might take place,
in which I can be, ideally, some little spark, some match light
in the mostly dark and empty universe, the thirteen dimensions of it, and my eternal match light would not necessarily require consciousness or lutes. And along with being this
spark, I can imagine that I have a tone, and if I were going
to pick one, I would pick something high in the treble clef,
something I couldn't reach when I was a baritone pretending to be a tenor. As this note, or some other note, I can
imagine a heaven where I get to play this tone, and to col-

lide with other notes, as if I were a constituent in a John
Cage piece, and here there are no entrances and exits, and I
don't have to have perfect rhythm, nor do I have to know
my scales, because I am all scales. Therefore I have no
responsibilities; as a note I just am, because I can't be entirely
eliminated, because that doesn't happen—energy gets
reused—and in this piece of music you can come in anywhere. You can be a part of it or not a part of it, and this
composition has a long duration, an eternal duration, but
you don't have to worry about this, because you are no
longer a perceiving entity. You are just the note and the note
is a good thing to be in this composition, which has all the
characteristics that good things have, namely it causes no
harm, and believes only in its iteration as goodness, which is
harmony and sublimity. And all kinds of other music are
apparent in this music, even though they are lost, all possible
music is contained in this infinite music, so Simon and
Garfunkel are there, and Funkadelic, and Arvo Pärt, maybe
even Rush, because everything is in there, and in this way I
am gone and gone is good, but I am also a very excellent
musician and no one is any better, except the artful arranger
of all sounds.

HOBBLING (WALKING, FLAPPING) NORTH

Cynthia Bourgeault

IN THE COMMON WAY of looking at things heaven is a place you go after you die (if you've been good). And I suppose that overall this shorthand is true: when the physical body has dissolved, there is less to obscure what had really been there all along anyway.

But it is possible to encounter heaven earlier, while still in physical flesh, and to live in it—and *from* it—here and now. In fact, more than a few people think that's exactly what Jesus meant by his term the *kingdom of heaven:* it's *this* world seen through the eyes and heart of divine love. Or perhaps better, it's the flood of transfiguring energy set loose in this world once the eyes of heaven have awakened.

So why not go for it now? For sure, this question stumped Jesus; you could even say it comprised the tragic miscalculation of his life. Why, when this angelically tinged "other" is as simple as opening the eyes of the heart here and now, why wouldn't people immediately open their eyes and give thanks? Why does the good news tend to receive a rain check?

But the fact is, this other way of seeing requires a high level of spiritual attunement—to use the current buzzword, *presence*—far more so than is accustomed or perhaps comfortable in this life. "Those who are given liberty by Him to act freely are nailed on the earth; and those who are free to act as they choose on the earth will be nailed in the heavens," an old Sufi proverb goes. One becomes a fastidious servant of the Now, not of daydreams and future options, and certainly not of one's personal preferences and agendas. It's a strange, Himalayan environment of the heart that seems out of tempo with most of what we usually call "getting the most out of life." And so heaven can wait, as the old saying goes. It's easier to get caught up in the enchantments and diversions of *this* existence. Drink it in for all it's worth, then allow heaven to be "next," once the veil has melted on its own.

That would have been my idea, too, twelve years ago. When I first met Raphael, my spiritual teacher at St. Benedict's Monastery, the collision of our hearts knocked us both off our feet, and for a while we wandered happily in the never-never land of being in love. We fixed up my old ranch house together, sipped cappuccino on the deck, and shared wonderful, rich conversations, heart pouring into heart. Even Rafe occasionally got seduced by the magic. "If this was ten years ago, I would have married you," he told me.

But it wasn't. It was now. He was seventy years old (twenty years my senior) and a Trappist monk in hermit's vows. He lived alone in a little cabin up in the hills above St. Benedict's Monastery in the Colorado Rocky Mountains, where he would repair for days and sometimes weeks on end to listen to the high angelic stirrings and attempt to fashion himself accordingly. Through that deeply habituated inner listening, he knew unwaveringly that there was a different trajectory in store for us. This would be the last gambit of his life, and it was not about households and cappuccino. From the moment he first took my hands after Mass at the monastery and declared his heart, he also announced the purpose of our time together was "to form a conscious connection that will last from here to eternity." That sounded romantic to me. For Rafe it wasn't. It was useful. Something God wanted. Something the planet needed. I'm not even sure, all things considered, that I'm the one he would have chosen, if it came to choosing in that usual romantic sense. But he knew that I was the one that God had sent around for this work, and that the window of opportunity was brief. For the year-and-a-half given to us we saw each other nearly every day and worked intensely together in what became a race against time to get me up to speed in the new configuration. "You have to find that part of you that already is beyond death and start to live out of that *now*," he insisted. His last teachings, as both of us marked his mysteriously rapid physical decline, were both tender and urgent. "You'll see, you'll see, nothing is taken away," were his final words to me, two days before the massive heart attack that ended his life.

Somewhere between student and widow, I stood in the back of the monastery chapel for his requiem mass, inconspicuous in a large crowd of mourners. The final lines of a poem by Theodore Roethke kept rattling around in my mind: "I, with no rights in the matter, neither father nor lover. . . ." If, during those final months of his life anyone had paid attention at all to Rafe's strange liaison with the tomboy-looking writer lady who encamped at his side and soaked up his wisdom like a sponge, now was certainly not the occasion to acknowledge it. Decked out in his full monastic regalia, Brother Raphael Robin was dispatched to his final resting place in the monastery graveyard amid the usual theological assurances that he had "finished his earthly work," "found what he was looking for," and was now free of all earthly

constraints. As for me—"Well, I suppose you'll be moving
on soon," everybody said.

That was pretty much my take, too, at first. I had promised Rafe, and God, that I would see his earthly life through,
but I'd pretty much expected that would be that. The promise of eternal connection he'd held out to me seemed just
too vast for me to wrap my mind around, and I still thought
it was mostly just his way of romantic talking. Once he was
gone, I supposed that I'd return to my former home in
Maine, find a new relationship, and get back into the stream
of my life. Following the usual way of looking at things, it
was time now for grief—and that other contemporary
buzzword, "closure."

It didn't dawn on me all at once that this was not going
to be the scenario. This other knowing unfolded only gradually, over several weeks, and it surprised me as much as anyone.

What stopped me initially from simply packing up my
household and getting on with my life was sheer respect for
Rafe. He had insisted that this was true, that we were to
form a union that endured beyond death; he had staked the
final years of his life on the reality of this mission and on trying to prepare me for it. If the things he stood for were true,
and if I loved him, then I needed to give it a chance. I felt
like I was his lineage bearer. For better or worse, he had
given his life trying to point me in the direction he was
looking. Out of love for him, I needed to keep on looking
there.

So I did, trying to work and live by the teachings he'd
given me. And to my astonishment and relief, the signs of his
continuing presence in my life were not long in coming.

About a month after his death I had a very vivid dream
confirming to me that I was on the right track. As the dream
opened, Rafe was the pilot of a small, cropduster-style
biplane, and I was awkwardly suspended on a trapeze hanging below it. Somehow we managed to take off in this con-

figuration, but then Rafe steered directly toward a huge concrete tower with an opening in the middle of it about thirty feet up. His plane managed to pass through the opening, but I on my trapeze fetched up on the ledge and watched him disappear off into the north.

What should I do? How was I ever going to get down? I tried awkwardly to flap my arms, and to my surprise, they carried me a little. I wasn't exactly flying, but they did break my fall, and I landed safely on the ground a few hundred yards beyond the tower. So I picked myself up and continued heading in the direction Rafe had vanished. Whenever there was a small hill or cliff, I'd climb it, flap my arms, and gain a few more miles to the north.

Finally, after what seemed like years of walking and flapping, hobbling north, I arrived at tavern in the Yukon, portentously named The Golden Spike. The whole scene was indeed bathed in golden light, and there was merry music coming from within the tavern. But following well-established procedure, I bypassed the music and climbed the outside stairs toward a second-story balcony. For what seemed like the thousandth time I jumped off, flapping my arms.

Suddenly, out of the far north, Rafe's little plane appeared again like a speck on the horizon; he swooped toward me and picked me up just before my feet hit the ground. But now the plane had two seats. I climbed in next to him, and together we flew off into that light.

Call it wish-fulfillment or call it mystical reassurance, that dream has pretty much been the story of these past twelve years. I keep hobbling along in the direction Rafe was traveling: figuratively jumping off cliffs, trying to flap my arms. I teach a bit, write a bit; I try to share with others the radiant and profoundly hopeful version of Christianity that he impressed into my heart. And in these efforts I ride the continuing updrafts of his spirit and feel his ground beneath my feet. But as I have gradually come to see, this is not so much because his love flows strong, but because his north is true.

Four years into the journey I published *Love Is Stronger than Death,* my first attempt to put words to my experience. In some ways it was probably not a smart or prudent move, for the book did part the waters of my life. But I felt like I needed to get the word out when I did, both to make contact with anyone else out there who might recognize what I was experiencing, and to try to row my small boat upstream against the floodtide of prevailing opinion that "Rafe's work was done," and that to continue in relationship was to "hold him back."

I had already seen repeatedly during those first four years of "griefwork" that most Christians, despite their theoretically "resurrection faith," actually have a very Old Testament understanding of death as a final separation, an irrevocable departure "down into the silence" (in the words of Psalm 115). Any traffic between the realms is seen as "necromancy." In the same vein, any soul who after death fails to make a clean break with the cares and concerns of this world can only be seen as a "ghost," a troubled being stuck between the universes. I can't tell you the number of times that people took umbrage at me for (as they saw it) implying that Rafe was such a troubled being; they simply could not compute what I was saying in any other category. "What about the communion of saints?" I suggested. "That's just for saints." For the normal lot of human beings, the dead "rest" and the living get on with their lives.

But that's not what Rafe believed, or what he taught me. His vision, echoing the ancient Wisdom traditions (which he immersed himself in during those long, solitary winters up at his cabin), was of an embedded hierarchy of realms, each interpenetrating and lifting each other up in a grand cosmic bootstrapping whose final goal is to reveal the glory of God in all its glowing fullness and intricate particularity. Far from being separated, the interface between these realms—"where the two seas meet," to use an old Wisdom metaphor—is the place where the glory shines most brightly, and one should do everything possible to dwell there at all times. Rafe believed firmly in what he called "the conscious circle of humanity," men and women both living and dead who during the time of this life have stabilized within themselves a very high level of spiritual consciousness. They become cosmic servants, working together across the realms as channels of divine mercy and compassion, and offering guidance—and occasional course corrections—to our dense and time-torn planet.

Like most high spiritual teachers, Rafe considered the act of dying to refer not to the death of one's physical body, but to the death of one's smaller or egoic self that keeps us fearful and imprisoned in our own skins, unable to reach out to the bottomless vastness of divine love. That's what he meant when he told me, "You must find that part of you that is already beyond death and begin to live out of it now." For those who in this life have truly managed to die ("dying before you die," in the classic spiritual terminology, or in Jesus' teaching, "losing your life in order to gain it"), the actual death of the physical body poses no disruption of one's identity. One simply maintains trajectory, fully alive and embodied in the glory itself.

Hence the double irony of our culture's current psychotherapeutic obsession with "griefwork" and "closure" following the death of a loved one. In the bolder and more visionary Christianity that Rafe taught me, not only is the continued walk with a human beloved beyond the grave possible, it is holy. Every couple whose love transcends death witnesses to the unbreakable interconnection of the realms and becomes part of the bright shining of heaven within our human midst.

To my delight, I discovered there were others out there who felt the same way. After *Love Is Stronger than Death* was published, I received a flood of mail thanking me for breaking the silence and putting into words what many have known and lived in the secrecy of their hearts. I now see that there is a whole band of lovers out there—mostly widows and widowers, but also parents for a child and children for a parent or grandparent—who for years and even decades have simply been silently going about their business of opening their hearts and living between the realms. It is not without reason that the early church listed "widows" in its ranks of angelic and holy beings, and why even now we single them out in our intercessory prayers. Theirs is a unique vocation, lived out (like all vocations) on behalf of and in solidarity with the entire human family.

Four years into the journey was still too early for me to have any real perspective on where the path might eventually be headed. Now that I've rounded the twelve-year mark, there's been enough water under the bridge to see the shape more clearly than I did at first, and the relationship with Rafe, while still going strong, has had time to undergo some distinct phases and transitions. Aware of my new friends out there who may be more recently embarked on this same path, let me reflect a little about what these phases have been like for me.

For the first two years, it was all about love. Despite what Rafe had tried to teach me about getting beyond romanticism, it was romanticism that sustained me as I adjusted to this new arrangement of being together invisibly. I stayed close to the monastery, sorted through his stuff up at the cabin, and learned to trust his presence in the new patterns of communication (mostly a palpable sense of touch, and instructions and assurances that seemed to appear in my heart out of nowhere). It was intensely personal, sometimes poignantly so. Steering by this new radar, I was able to find my way to his old family home in Louisiana and discover details of his tragic childhood; in gentler moments he would show up, like any good husband, to help me move a table or change a tire. "We're touching right now!" he used to tell me in the early days of our romance when we would speak on the phone together, training me even then to prefer the touch of the heart to the touch of hands and legs. Our new life was simply an extension of that training. Alone and grief-stricken, I had to begin to learn and trust that I was neither alone nor grief-stricken. Like any other lover, I thought Rafe loved me because I was special, and I kept reciting the litany of our specialness as the evidence that the love would continue. Only slowly did I come to see it was the other way around.

Gradually we allowed the tether to widen, and the kites flew farther out. In the next phase, which lasted for about seven years, the scene shifted both outwardly and inwardly. I moved away from the monastery and began a new career in British Columbia. But more than that, I began to realize that the sphere of our "touching" came most intensely when I was in service to others: teaching, leading meditation retreats, building a new organization, The Contemplative Society, with a dedicated and growing group of people. More and more my teaching moved away from what I'd learned "by the books," and into what I was learning through the ongoing journey with Rafe. And it was during these times, when I knew more than I knew and shared it with a heart afire, that our continuing partnership was most radiant, both inwardly and outwardly visible.

In these most recent years, I see yet another shift under-way. My life has once again reinvented itself physically; I'm now mostly back in Maine, writing and living the hermit's life as Rafe taught it to me, occasionally stirring out for teaching and retreat work. And in that deepening silence I notice that more and more our story has begun to fade into the one story; the Mystery of love itself. It's as if, having waited all these years for that "happy ending" to my dream—Rafe returning in his biplane and scooping me aboard—I find that it honestly no longer matters. To have walked, flapped, and hopped this far is enough in itself; the journey itself reveals the full curvature of the heart. Whether

I see him again or not in some grand reunion on my
deathbed, what we have done stands in its own ground.

I know what I've just said may sound anticlimactic: after
all *this,* to simply let go and let it all fade away? But as the
poet Philip Booth once wisely put it, "How you get there is
where you'll arrive." I know how Rafe and I got here, and
I have some inkling of where we're arriving. Finally, I think,
I'm fully ready to hear the profound and challenging truth
he'd been trying to share with me all along.

During his last year up at the cabin, Rafe had been quite
taken with a quatrain from Shakespeare's Sonnet number 73
(the "bare ruined choirs" sonnet). He copied it out by hand
and pinned it up above his prayer desk:

> In me thou see'st the glowing of such fire
> That on the ashes of his youth doth lie,
> As the death-bed whereon it must expire,
> Consumed with that which it was nourished by.

I supposed at first that he was simply identifying with the
persona in that poem: an old man in the midst of a hopeless
love. But Rafe saw more; it was the "consumed with that
which he was nourished by" line that galvanized him, cap-
turing in a single image the entire meaning and purpose of
his life. He understood that our real business here on earth
is to become "all flame." A candle is not a candle until it
burns, but only wick and tallow. Just so, he saw, our life here
on earth is merely wick and tallow; only when set aflame—
by conscious striving and self-immolating love—does it
reveal its true purpose and destiny. And whenever and wherever this happens, eternity is present. Rafe knew this with all
his heart; it was the core of his visionary mysticism. And he
gladly offered up the wick and tallow of his human life to
the holocaust of his transfiguration.

I suspect this was the core of Jesus' visionary mysticism as
well, and certainly at the heart of his notion of the kingdom
of heaven. For when you really think about it, this kingdom

he spoke about so often and insistently is accessed not by dying, but rather by *living:* living with such radical generosity, self-abandonment, and open-endedness to eternity that we become part of the continuing alchemy through which love makes itself known. And when this happens, we know that the same "love that moves the stars and the sun" (as Dante called it) flows also in us and in everything, tying together worlds both seen and unseen in a single, intricate tapestry of mutual yearning and blessing. Nothing is ever lost from it, but nothing ever remains the same.

And so it's no surprise that Rafe and Cynthia are disappearing into the flame, the love story "consumed with that which it was nourished by." But the love itself, to the extent that it remains a trajectory of the divine Mercy, is a fire of heaven, burning on the dark shores of this world.

MOMENTS IN THIN PLACES

Malcolm Boyd

"OUR FATHER IN HEAVEN, hallowed be your Name, your kingdom come, your will be done, on earth as in heaven." Here is heaven in the beginning of the Lord's Prayer. I start every morning praying it.

While heaven is a cornerstone of my life, I can't pinpoint it on an existing map. Is it hidden in the frozen Arctic or tucked into an area northeast of Baku, a forgotten valley of Easter Island or a secret monastic community in the world's remotest desert? One can't procure a government visa to visit it. So it curiously bears a certain resemblance to the phenomenon called Hollywood, which novelist Nathanael West noted is not so much a place as a state of mind. By the same token, heaven isn't a place on a map, a prized piece of religious real estate, or developer's dream.

Can we say it is God's home? I prefer to perceive it "through a glass darkly" as what I might call God's holiest of holies. What is my connection, if any, to heaven? I've seen glimpses of it only by eyes of faith. I've felt the presence—never in a merely logical way—in thin places or passages that I've encountered on occasion between the visible world and—what? Greater reality? God's love and power? Awareness of the holy?

Ten days before her ninety-ninth birthday, my mother lay dying. I was with her in the convalescent hospital where she'd resided for the past four-plus years. Beatrice appeared to be unconscious. I held her limp hand in mine.

Suddenly, a change occurred. Her hand gripped mine with fierce strength. Now her eyes opened, staring directly into mine with a determination, even a passion, that was startling. I grasped her hand, held her gaze. Then, after a moment, her eyes closed. Shortly her grip wavered and let go.

I knew Beatrice had left and gone to heaven. I could almost follow her journey into what seemed to be light. Her departure was not passive, nor had her life been. In Beatrice there burned an intensity. Born in 1898, she had always lived in what used to be referred to as "a man's world." While accepting its Spartan rules, she kept inviolate a part of her life that was a "secret garden." So, as a single mom who had to work, she did so during her days. But, in her private time, she painted and sketched and gardened. Fame did not touch her; she had no interest in it. Her honesty could be almost shocking in its directness. She remained open to life, clearly honoring the moment at hand.

Hanging on a wall of my house is a painting of lilacs. Beatrice is the artist. I remember when she did it. I was in my early teens. I also grasped the fact Beatrice was secretly in love with another artist, a well-known one. He was married, Beatrice was divorced, the relationship was never mentioned. In fact, it didn't surface. But kids know things like that. It was a brief encounter, a fleeting moment of sensitivity between two people. So, as I understood well Beatrice's fierce determination and strong commitment in meeting life's harsh demands, yet I was granted an opportunity to quietly observe her compelling vulnerability and heartfelt response to flesh and spirit.

Being with Mother on the occasion—at the very moment—of her journey's end here, and the start of her

journey to heaven, was a deeply touching revelation of
God's mercy, healing, and treasured gift of this thin place
close to heaven.

It was the summer of 1965. As a volunteer worker for black
voter registration in the Deep South, I lived with four young
men, all of them African American veterans of the civil rights
movement. One had been sentenced once to a chain gang
for a civil rights–related offense. All had experiences of jails,
police brutality, and rejection by white society.

At the outset they told me, "We can't make it with a
white this close for this long a time. You're not Negro. But
you're going to have to be a nigger with us." This meant we
slept on shack floors (one night a snake crept up through a
hole and had to be killed), ate only when poor black families shared food with us, and our safety was constantly under
duress and cruel threat. In fact, I was reminded of J. B.
Priestley's classic definition of hell. "Hell—not fiery and
romantic but grey, greasy, dismal—is just around the corner."

I remember a Sunday morning when I wished to attend
a church service. But where? I would jeopardize a black
church if, as an identifiable white "outside agitator," I publicly entered its space. Of course, I would be outrageously
unwelcome—a symbol of controversy and possible violence—if I attempted to enter a white church. Yet the issue
was deeper, for how could I leave behind my companions in
order to meet God inside any building that was closed to
them?

A wobbly wooden table provided our altar in the shack
where we'd spent the night. Bread near moldy and warm
beer provided sacramental elements. The old shack itself
became a thin place as we celebrated the Eucharist. In my
mind's eye I saw a heavenly choir providing choral music,
while the tower of a great cathedral sheltered us above.

On May 16, 2004, Bishop J. Jon Bruno of Los Angeles blessed the union of Mark Thompson and myself—two gay men—celebrating the twentieth year of our life partnership. The Cathedral Center of St. Paul, the locus of the ritual, seemed an outpost of heaven as vows were exchanged.

> Mark and Malcolm, do you believe God has called
> you into a life-long covenant of love and fidelity?
> *We do believe.*
> Will you live together in love?
> *We will, with God's help.*
> Will you be faithful to one another?
> *We will, with God's help.*
> Will you support one another in love so that you
> may grow into maturity of faith in Jesus Christ?
> *We will, with God's help.*
> Will you do all in your power to make your life
> together a witness to the love of God in the world?
> *We will, with God's help.*

Then each of us said to the other in turn:

> *I give myself to you. I love you, trust you, and delight in*
> *you. I will share your burdens and your joys, for richer or*
> *poorer, in sickness and in health, until we are parted by*
> *death. I will go with you wherever God calls us. This is my*
> *solemn promise.*

In that moment heaven was not at all a distant location in my life or a place "above." It seemed very close. Holiness enveloped the scene in warmth and light. A number of different parts of my life melded together wondrously in graceful, simple, ordinary, and remarkable ways.

WHEN HEAVEN HAPPENS
Margaret Bullitt-Jonas

CATCH ME IN A certain mood, and I have no use for heaven. When a cold wind blows through my soul, I store up complaints like root vegetables against a hard winter.

Belief in heaven is outdated. We've outgrown those boring angels playing harps on puffy clouds.

Heaven is foolish wish-fulfillment, the fantasy of a happy afterlife.

Heaven is an illusion meant to distract us from the disappointments and suffering of this life.

Heaven is a blank screen upon which we project whatever we want.

Who needs heaven? I can do without it.

That's what I declare in bitter times. Anger propels such thoughts, and a sorrow that slides toward despair, for what torments me most is the sense that heaven is here and we're taking it down.

Heaven is under our feet as well as over our heads—that's what Thoreau said. And I believe it. But how can I bear to perceive the heaven here at hand when we're killing the living glory that surrounds us? Clear-cut forests. Disappearing topsoil. Melting glaciers. Drowning polar bears. Growing deserts. Dying coral. What meaning can heaven have when a quarter of the world's species may be committed to extinction?

In times of despair I tell myself that hope in heaven is naïve. I make my case against heaven and protect myself from its lure. I harden my heart, congratulate myself on facing facts, and refuse to be seduced by hope.

The trouble is, I can't keep it up for long. My litany of complaint omits what matters most: the fact that heaven comes upon me, nevertheless. If we dare to long for heaven and to take a stand for its possibility, strange things can happen. Who knows? We might find ourselves at the bottom of a jail cell in Washington, D.C., with heaven itself coming to pay a visit. That is what happened to me.

A few years ago, during an Easter service at a suburban church near Boston, I listened as the preacher paced the aisle and preached his homily. Jesus had risen, he told us. The stone had moved, and an angel was sitting triumphantly on top.

"Do you know what we're going to do?" he asked. "Tonight we're going to move some stones." He paused, as if to roll up his sleeves and gather strength for the task ahead.

"What kind of stones are in front of you?" Steven went on. "Every person is up against some kind of stone. Is it money you're worried about? Is it your health? Are you worried about your child? What is the stone that is lying on your heart?"

I watched a few parishioners wipe their eyes: a young woman whose husband was dying, another whose cancer was incurable. I could think of no stones of my own—no health problems, no financial strain, no relationships in distress. But then something began to roll before my eyes, something massive and weighty that stopped just inches from my face and refused to move. I recognized it with a sinking heart. It was the stone of the environmental crisis. And not only that—it was my own despair. Sure, I voted for candidates who cared about conservation and renewable resources. I bought organic and locally grown food. I avoided Styrofoam and recycled with the best of them. But what difference did that make? The Bush administration was in power, and news of the environment was getting worse every day. What could I possibly do to protect the Earth? What could any of us do? Quite likely it was too late to do anything.

"I have stones, too," Steven was saying. "It gets dark in the tomb sometimes. I need you to join me. We have to do this together. Will you pray with me? Can we move the stones together?"

I closed my eyes.

"Come, Lord Christ," he prayed. "I'm trapped in this tomb. It gets so dark, I can hardly see. I hardly know where I am. Without your help, I can't get out."

In his words I heard a cry for liberation, the cry of every living creature that longs for life.

Yes, I prayed. *That's right.*

Prayer has a way of clarifying desire. I remembered the tadpole I'd seen at our pond in western Massachusetts. It was a tiny thing, but as I watched it, a wild, loving longing rose up in me. I wanted that tadpole to live. My fierce hunger to protect the natural world focused on that little speck of life. Maybe if that tadpole lived, then so, too, would the birch tree leaning at the water's edge, and the red-winged blackbird gliding overhead. If that tadpole lived, then maybe the network of life into which it had been hatched was still intact, still shining and resilient. Maybe it could still be saved.

So I brought the tadpole with me into prayer, and the birch tree and blackbird. Together we prayed for light and looked for some way out.

"Help us, dear Christ. We put our trust in you. We love you. Give us strength to roll away the stone."

I felt something shift inside me. I knew what I had to do. I had to go to Washington. A new coalition of clergy and laypeople from a range of religious traditions was gathering

in D.C. to express its concern about global climate change
and to hold a prayer vigil against oil drilling in the Arctic
National Wildlife Refuge. They called themselves Religious
Witness for the Earth. I needed to join them, perhaps even
risk arrest. If I wanted to bear witness to the Christ who
bursts from the tomb, if I wanted to bear witness to the
Christ who proclaims that life, not death, has the last word,
then it was time to put my faith on the line.

At the end of the prayer, the room fell silent. Steven lifted
his head and looked around.

"Did you feel the stone move? Maybe it budged only
this much," he said, smiling as he held thumb and forefinger
an inch apart, no bigger than a tadpole. "But that's something. That's a start. Some of those stones are really big."

Opening my heart to heaven was the first step. Taking my
stand for heaven was the second. A few weeks after the
Easter Vigil service, I traveled to Washington to meet the
members of Religious Witness. On the first day we learned
about oil drilling and the Arctic, about climate change and
fossil fuels. On the second we lobbied our members of
Congress and studied the disciplines of nonviolent civil dis-
obedience. On the third about a hundred of us marched
down Independence Avenue in religious vestments, carrying
banners and singing. We made our way through a garden
that yielded a glimpse of iris and azalea, and stepped back
onto the sidewalk.

I looked ahead. Across the street loomed the Department
of Energy, an enormous structure made of stone. It rose
before my eyes, impenetrable, implacable, and surrounded by
police. Stationed alongside the building were four police
vans, half-a-dozen cruisers, and some forty officers. Police
photographers stood in doorways and on benches, taking
pictures of us from every angle.

I was startled. Were they expecting a riot? An angry crowd of thousands?

We *should* have been thousands—that's what *I* thought, anyway. Surely we represented thousands of people and millions of other species. But that morning the disparity in power could not have been starker. Our little group had no weapons, no backup forces, not even the time of day: expecting arrest, we had brought nothing with us, no wallet, handbag, or keys, not even a watch.

Still, the "Alleluia" we sang did not falter. Carried by its sound, we moved into the plaza and formed a circle for a brief prayer service. In the shadow of the building's overhang we asked God to forgive our complicity in excessive consumption, waste, and pollution. We prayed for government policies that respect the sacredness of the Earth. We gave thanks for the beauty of Creation, and expressed sorrow for the ways we were destroying it. I read a lament written by a group from the United Nations and was haunted by its sad refrain, "We have forgotten who we are."

The minister stepped forward to deliver a homily. The natural world was deteriorating, he said. In years to come our children and grandchildren would ask us the same awful question that was asked after the abolition of slavery and after the fall of the Third Reich: "How could you not have known? Knowing what you knew, how could you have failed to act?"

That's right, I whispered. *Today we're going to move a stone.*

The worship service was coming to an end. We sang "Amazing Grace," and then the twenty-two of us who had decided to risk arrest walked slowly to the doors of the Department of Energy.

I felt us cross an invisible boundary. With the others, I stepped over a threshold I could not see. I walked out of my ordinary life.

I am neither a law-breaker nor a thrill-seeker. More often than not, I follow the rules—even enforce them. I fasten my seatbelt, don't cheat on taxes, write thank you notes, and stand up when the band plays our national anthem. But here I was, intentionally and publicly breaking the law. As if some inner revolution had quietly taken place, the old "me" was no longer in charge. Whatever security I'd felt in operating within the rules was gone. That's partly why I felt so frightened as I left the safety of the circle and moved toward the door: I hardly recognized myself. I hardly knew who I was.

We stand or kneel in prayer, our backs to the building. The pavement under my knees is hard. At home, I often sit on a meditation cushion to pray. Today there is no cushion, just the weight of my body against stone. I lift up my hands. I'm dressed for the Eucharist. I might as well hold out my arms as I do at the Eucharist.

Instead of pews filled with parishioners, I see ranks of police and a cluster of supporters. I am afraid. I've never been arrested before. Years ago, as a VISTA volunteer in Mayor Rizzo's Philadelphia, I heard innumerable stories of police brutality. It's not that I really expect the same thing to happen to me—the punch in the gut, the assault behind closed doors. Still, my body tenses as I place myself against the cops, the Feds, the law.

I close my eyes. One by one we pray aloud, words thrown into space, words hurled against stone.

Is this whole thing ridiculous? I briefly open my eyes and notice a well-dressed man watching us. He strokes his tie, leans over, and says something to a fellow nearby. The two of them chuckle. I have no idea what they're talking about, but I wonder if they think we look absurd. I suppose we do. Here we are with our jerry-rigged signs, our predictably earnest songs and prayers of protest, a foolhardy band straight out of the sixties.

Defensively, I imagine confronting that mocking man with the arsenal of our credentials. *We're no rag-tag bunch,* I want to tell him. *We're people with doctorates and master's degrees—nurses and ministers, writers and accountants. Thoughtful people, educated people, professionals.*

I am distracted from prayer by this indignant outburst. *Let it go,* wisdom tells me. *None of that matters—your degrees, your skills, your status in the world. The privileges of race and class mean nothing now. You're a woman on your knees, that's who you are—one human being pleading with God.*

I turn my attention back to prayer and continue to stretch out my arms. Suddenly I realize that behind the tension, behind the fear and self-consciousness, something else is welling up. I am jubilant.

Lift up your hearts, I might as well be saying to the people before me, beaming as broadly as I do at the Eucharist.

We lift them to the Lord, would come the response.

How did I miss it? After years of going to church, after years of celebrating the Eucharist, only now, as I kneel on pavement and face a phalanx of cops, do I understand so clearly that praising God can be an act of political resistance. That worship is an act of human liberation. The twenty-two of us come from different faith traditions, but each of us is rooted in a reality that transcends the rules and structures of this world. Tap into that transcendent truth, let the divine longing for a community of justice and mercy become your own deepest longing, and who knows what energy for life will be released?

I feel as defiant as a maple seedling that pushes up through asphalt. It is God I love, and God's green Earth. I want to bear witness to that love even in the face of hatred or indifference, even if the cost is great.

So what if our numbers are small? So what if, in the eyes of the police, in the eyes of the world, we have no power? I'm beginning to sense the power that is ours to wield, the power of self-offering. We may have nothing else, but we do have this, the power to say, "This is where I stand. This is what I love. Here is something for which I'm willing to put my body on the line."

I never knew that stepping beyond the borders of what I find comfortable could make me so happy. That shifting from self-preservation to self-offering could awaken so much joy.

Is it heaven that we glimpse in such moments of self-offering? Is this what Jesus meant when he promised that the poor in spirit and those who hunger and thirst for righteousness would receive the kingdom of heaven? It seems that way to me, though of course I can't be sure. But heaven wasn't done showing me a thing or two that day.

After blocking the doors of the Energy Department we were arrested, handcuffed, photographed, locked into a van, and driven to a holding cell. There we were frisked, photographed, herded back into the van, and driven to a second jail. With the other women I passed a tedious afternoon stuffed into a nine-by-nine-foot cell with a single metal bunk. Late in the day, by now hungry, weary, and struggling to keep up our spirits, we were handcuffed for the third time and led into the van. Surely at any moment we would be released. Surely the guards were taking us somewhere that led back to the outside world.

Instead, when the van door opened, we were escorted across an underground parking lot and into a basement. As I passed through the metal detector, I caught a glimpse of a narrow corridor lined with cells. D.C.'s Central Holding Block is a windowless, self-enclosed underworld, and everything is painted green—not the vibrant green of a healthy forest, but a sickly hue, the color of yellowing grass as it dies under a rock.

A guard frisked me and inked my fingerprints.

"This way," she said curtly, hustling me down the corridor. Our group was separated into individual cells. Confused, I heard the heavy door close behind me with a clang. I was locked with another protester named Sally in a four-by-six-foot cubicle furnished with two sheet-metal bunks. No pillow, no mattress, no window, nothing but a toilet without a seat. The floor was filthy. I didn't want to touch anything. What suffering had this "holding block" held? How much misery and rage, the wreckage of how many lives? I'd never been in a walled-up place that spoke so grimly of lovelessness and despair.

"Was it stupid to get into this situation?" Sally demanded. I wished I knew. What the hell were we doing here? We'd expected to be released hours ago. Were we being harassed or was this just the slow grind of bureaucracy?

Sally and I moved restlessly about. She perched on the bottom bunk and I climbed up on top. Illegible names and symbols had been scratched into the greenish paint, traces of previous occupants. I wondered what sharp tool they had found to etch the fact of their existence on these metal slates. I had nothing but the clothes on my back, plus fingernails and teeth. What mark would *I* leave? What mark can *any* of us leave in this world before we die?

I heard an insistent voice from the bunk below. "What have we accomplished by getting arrested? Can you tell me one person whose mind we changed because of our protest this morning?"

I peered over the edge of the bunk, annoyed. I didn't want to hear this. I was trying to hold myself together and Sally was undercutting my resolve. How would I handle my hunger and anxiety if our arrest had no meaning?

Give me a break, I wanted to say.

"Did we change the mind of one policeman?" she continued relentlessly. "The mind of one passerby? What difference does it make that we prayed for environmental justice and got arrested? So what?"

Sally was a leader in environmental activism in the church, used to producing tangible results. Just now I hated her for voicing my own thoughts. What good was it to be locked up in this God-forsaken cell? Why were we here? What was the point?

I kept a stony silence and stared grimly at the wall. My mind went back to when I knelt in prayer on the pavement with my arms outstretched. How long ago that moment seemed, how poignant the gesture. In retrospect, it seemed as lovely and fragile as a flower. What is the point of a flower? It has no point. It leaves no mark—it just expresses beauty. It is what it is, without power to compel response.

"Oh, Sally," I said. "I don't know. I hope our vigil and arrest made a difference to someone. Of course I want to be effective and do what I can to protect the Earth. But sometimes all we can do is bear witness to what we love."

I thought of the wise teachers I'd read—Thomas Merton, Mother Teresa, Henri Nouwen—who urge us to focus on being faithful, not successful.

"Sometimes all we can do is sow a seed," I said. "And hand the results to God."

I tried to believe what I was saying. Being faithful just then was no small task. It felt presumptuous even to say the word "God" in this abandoned place, as if in this pit the word was empty, signifying nothing. I felt trapped inside myself, unable to pray. What if there was nothing but these walls, nothing but this anxiety and despair? What if the silence of the world was filled not with divinity but with nothing at all? What if heaven was a fantasy, and hell was all there was?

Late that night a guard appeared with the first food we had seen since the morning's arrest: stacks of cellophane-wrapped bologna sandwiches and donuts. Another guard held up pink Kool-Aid in Styrofoam cups.

I was hungry, but I don't eat meat and I can't eat sugar. I accepted a couple of bologna sandwiches through the slot in the bars, unwrapped the cellophane, and peeled off a slice of bread. I asked for some water.

I looked wanly at the meal. Well, never mind, it made sense: jail food. Bread and water.

"Watch out," called Kate from the opposite cell. "The bread is moldy."

Recoiling, I peered at the slice of bread. I could see nothing gray, but it was too dark to get a good look. I took a little bite of the loathsome stuff, intending to gulp it down fast so I wouldn't notice my disgust.

But as the bread touched my tongue, I paused, remembering the Eucharist, how Jesus gives himself to us in the bread and the wine. My disgust vanished, along with my sense of deprivation. I took a second, slow bite of the bread, and ate it with reverence. I took a slow sip of water. To my astonishment, I saw that everything I needed was here. As I patiently consumed the bread and water, my anxiety slipped away. I was at peace. I knew I was free. It didn't matter that I was still in jail. It didn't matter that I had no idea when I'd get out. None of that mattered. I felt fed from within, as if a river of joy were secretly flowing through me.

I looked around my cell, amazed. Everything was exactly the same—the same bleak walls and metal bunk, the same rows of bars. Nothing had budged. The world around me was still solid and real. But everything had changed. It was as if my outward circumstances had fallen away, or as if they had filled with some hidden radiance. Everything material seemed to open to something beyond itself, to be secretly as spacious as the Arctic wilderness, as suffused with light.

I almost burst out laughing. *They think they've imprisoned me, but I'm already free!*

I looked at Sally: she was lying on the bottom bunk. Grabbing the other bologna sandwich still wrapped in plastic, I climbed back onto the top bunk and lay down. I tried out Sally's suggestion and discovered that she was right: the sandwiches made a great pillow.

Very softly, I began to sing, "Alleluia, alleluia, give thanks to the Risen Lord"—an Easter hymn, one of my favorites.

Sally hummed along. What a pleasure to feel her companionship as we praised God in these familiar words and
melody. Who would have guessed the acoustics would be so
good?

Someday, I grinned to myself, *when swords are beaten into
plowshares, this cellblock will make a great music studio. My husband's bamboo flute would sound heavenly in here.*

Sally stood up and leaned against the bars.

"Hey," she called discreetly into the corridor, but loudly
enough so that the rest of our group could hear. "Do you
think that now would be a good time to ask the guards not
to use Styrofoam?"

I heard a roar of laughter.

I can explain why heaven makes no sense, why the most
logical response to the human condition is despair, why the
future that lies ahead of us is only chaotic and dark, why
we—as individuals, as a species, as a planet—in fact have no
future at all. I can explain why belief in heaven as afterlife or
belief in heaven on earth is equally impossible, equally
absurd. But eventually, and often when I least expect it,
something in me rises up and declares: Nevertheless. Is it the
Risen Christ? That's what I would say. For when it comes,
so does heaven—a glimpse of it, anyway, a chink in the wall,
an echo in the ear. And hope becomes possible again, a hope
as lovely and startling as the sight of Earth rising above the
barren landscape of the moon.

WHO KNOWS WHO GETS TO GO?

Benjamin Morse

BACK IN 1982 MY parents had arranged for a young curate to visit our house on St. Francis Day and bless our dog, four cats, two rabbits, and two goldfish. After he left, my sister and I wore the longest of faces. My mother didn't miss a beat when we told her the devastating news—that according to him animals do not go to heaven. "Maybe not in the part of heaven *he's* going to," she clarified, "but don't you worry. All of our pets will definitely go to heaven. Only no one will be allergic to them, and they won't have fleas."

I now realize that my mother, soon to be at divinity school, was in fact waxing exegetical on some of Isaiah's eschatological imagery, and I don't think she was entirely humoring us either. If lions and lambs can lie down together, then surely even parasites achieve their independence and refrain from being pests in paradise. The rabbis, I assume, would have extrapolated as much in the Midrash.

Prior to this spiritual turning point, I remember pondering the presence of electronics on the other side when my mother told me that after they die some people sometimes see their lives flash before them as if on a television screen. And on a trip ventured under the premise of greeting my father as his submarine docked at various harbors along his Mediterranean tour of duty, renderings by medieval and Renaissance masters and the portals surrounding cathedral doors helped imprint the traditional Western schematic configuration of heaven and hell on my young mind. So I prayed earnestly to God not to let me end up like one of those poor hollowed out souls who went screaming head-first into the burning jaws of hell.

At twenty-three I lost my mother, my only sibling, and two grandparents, but I had a sure sense that they had passed into a better life. Friends gave me books on tape about angels and near-death experiences as well as bestselling books by psychics with commercial smiles. Such titles once or twice seduced me in my grief, but the intrusion of right-wing doctrines (for example, "This is why God does not want there to be abortion, because the soul is not allowed to undertake its journey of learning about life and love") did not exactly scream of unclouded revelation.

Since following in my mother's footsteps and pursuing a doctorate in Old Testament/Tanakh, I should have something theologically concrete to say about where I think, feel, and hope their souls have gone. But "proof" has come mostly in the form of dream visitations, and I've clung to testimonies of friends and family who have witnessed people going up into the light. What lies on that other side, I imagine, is too wonderful for me to fathom or articulate. It defies religious or scriptural descriptions—our constructions of light and goodness, the uncanny or the numinous, the ineffable union with the eternal and the sublime, or any old mixture of mystical speak.

I have witnessed heaven in experiencing the tragic beauty of grace through grief. I have witnessed it at the ballet, in Ad Reinhart paintings, from our family porch, and even through reading critical theory and biblical criticism. Yet to talk about it openly is something I have grown increasingly uncomfortable with over the years, especially since I moved to the staunchly secular United Kingdom. I used to tell quite a few people about my dreams and how real they felt, but I am more protective of these experiences now. Explaining them and persuading someone that they're real makes them sound potentially false. Preserving them in the mind keeps them pure. Maybe this is partly why people have to pass death away with euphemism and with cotton-ball clouds and pearly gates. Death and heaven have to be talked around.

Ten years after my mother and sister died, there was little time to contemplate the passing of my father. I managed to write and recite a homily for his memorial services, but as the executor of his estate I had few spare moments to grieve in the months that followed. Returning to Glasgow from America six weeks after his death, I clicked onto an image on the *New York Times* website of a group kneeling in prayer on someone's front lawn. My first reaction to the image was naively positive: how amazing, I thought, they're praying for the poor woman and her husband. But when I read the article and realized these people were in fact protesting in front of Michael Schiavo's house, my rage at the hypocritical faithful surged. How could they condemn a suffering man on his own property for helping his wife out of her misery and into the light of Christ? And why was it, I asked myself, that Christians like this were so adamantly opposed to the loss of mortal life when there is the promise of life eternal? As an aunt of mine put it, "The very folks who ought to understand the concept of eternal life are the most determined not to let a dear soul pass on."

I also asked myself what it was these Christians were praying for. The fact that Terry Schiavo's condition originated from anorexia made me wonder. My sister had been anorexic for a year before she escaped from her hospital, swam across a river, and died of exposure several hundred yards along on the opposite bank. Following the funeral, one or two sources informed me that people were muttering about her probably not making it to heaven.

So it occurred to me that one reason conservative Christians were praying so hard for Terry was because they thought she didn't have a chance in heaven of making it there on her own. Anorexia, many insist, is like a form of suicide—a self-murder that constitutes an act against God. The cause of death on my sister's death certificate reads "suicide" in blunt typeface, but that doesn't tell the story of someone who crossed her own Red Sea when she made her flight and watched her demons drown like Egyptians in the river behind her. It simply eludes me how anyone could look at her death—or the death of Terry Schiavo—and pronounce there to be a problem with her eligibility for heaven. I can't imagine what compels someone to think like that about people burdened by sadness and illness to their ends.

Fear of death is what fuels "culture of life" advocates in their quest to control other people's lives. Abortion, suicide, and assisted death all apparently shut souls off from the possibility of heaven, but the logic behind such principles reflects what a failure death is to Christians today despite their belief in the afterlife. The "culture of life" campaign excludes, of course, compassion for people on death row and public recognition of Iraqi civilian death counts. Yet while all of those unilateralist religious politicians are shaking their heads at where they know liberals like me are going to go when the Day of Judgment comes, I'm wondering from my side if neoconservatives like them can ever make it to heaven. Can I guarantee that my own leftist neo-prophetic faith is one God will consider more noble than the evangelist's sinisterly repressed agenda? Can anyone be so sure it all ends in a fork in the road between a determinable good and bad, when God's ways are so different from our ways?

My father didn't seem to doubt that my sister had been welcomed into the light, but his views on the Schiavo case

were the opposite of mine. He wanted if possible to be kept
on life-support indefinitely. I have told my partner that if
I'm ever in that situation, if things don't look like they're
getting any better after two weeks or so, it's okay to let me
go whenever he sees fit. After all, what else is there after life
but more life?

In the minutes before my mother died, I was in the hospital room alone with her. I realized that maybe we were
giving up on her too soon, that maybe if I told her we still
believed in her survival she would be able to fight herself
back to recovery. I did so but also told her that if God was
calling her now, it was all right to let go. That final moment
together of living through sacred time, those minutes of
goodbye and thanksgiving, indeed showed me a glimpse of
heaven.

Ten days later I was back in New York speaking to my
sister on the phone and apologizing for having to postpone
the four-hour return journey required to visit her in her
ward until the next evening. She assured me she would be
okay, as if ready for the hereafter she would enter into the
following morning. Six months later she encircled me while
I was sleeping, hugged me, and delivered her farewell words.
She subsequently made her presence known in subtle but
certain ways.

I was on the other side of the ocean from my father
when he had his final heart attack, and our political differences had broadened a gulf induced by living far away from
one another. Almost a year on I finally got my dream visitation, in which he sang goodbye to me via a DVD he played
of himself performing a comedic (and highly professional)
Cole Porter sequence. Further evidence of electronics in the
next world, I suppose.

Today I remain ever wary of saying too many things on
heaven, and I have probably said enough here for a lifetime.
Except I can also tell you what I wouldn't mind it being
like: sailing with my parents and sister down the Niantic

River to our old house in Connecticut and having a big family reunion to include ancestors I never met and the natives who once lived on the peninsula there; casual banter with my mother, Joseph Albers, and Judith Butler about Nijinsky in a carved gothic library lined with ornamental covers by Owen Jones; my partner Richard playing Beethoven in one room and iTunes in another. And of course all of our family pets will be there, only they won't scratch the upholstery.

HOW I KNOW WHAT I KNOW

Maggie Robbins

ON THE TABLE NEXT to her bed in the condominium she shared with my grandfather in Bethesda, my mother's mother kept a slim, red paperback: *A Catholic's Ripley's Believe It or Not!* It was there every time I visited, every December and every June, along with a holder for spectacles and a little mat for a water glass. Despite their strained reticence on the subject, I had a pretty good idea that, if asked, my grandmother would come down on the side of believing it and my mother on the side of not; they had an ongoing whisper argument about bringing me to talk to my grandmother's priest in case I got sick again. I had no idea whether I believed it or didn't; I had no idea what *it* was.

I was not excited about the prospect of meeting a priest, yet I had questions I needed answered by religion. There seemed no practicable strategy: if I took the book to read, either my mother would see me with it or my grandmother would notice it was missing. Things were tense enough what with my institute checkups. One June afternoon, though, on a day when according to both my grandmother and my mother the weather wasn't warm enough for swimming, I finally sneaked the book off the bedside table and into one of the walk-in closets.

The cover claimed that the more than 475 facts the volume contained were all true. To me that sounded like research findings—what I had been seeking for several years, ever since I had been able to handle chapter books on my own. I was familiar with the concept of research; I knew I was presently in some. I read the *Ripley's* straight through, skipping not a single fact. I had never known that when St. Agnes, at age twelve, was stripped in the public square, the only man who did not avert his eyes was struck blind on the spot. Or that St. Barbara's executioner was killed by lightning immediately after he chopped off her head. Or that the air conditioning in the St. Louis cathedral had cost $360,000 to install. The book said that Jean Fabre, a Catholic, had been known as "the Homer of the Insect World." Whatever that could possibly mean.

What I wanted, however, was information about the afterlife, and especially about whether people can reverse themselves out of it, and the book had little to say on that topic. In fact, it included no facts about hell at all, and the only fact concerning heaven was "Souls in Heaven not only are excluded from suffering, but also have the ability to move with the speed of thought." I had no conception of how fast thought traveled—I still don't—and was more than shaky when it came to a definition of the soul. The use of the word *suffering* in that context seemed odd, as if it were a club. (My grandmother had told me that what I didn't know about religion would fill a book. It was true: I was ten before I knew *Christ* wasn't his last name.) So I had done all that reading for nothing.

The following day, though, downstairs, while my grandfather was asleep in his deck chair next to the pool, I saw a woman sitting at the patio table over by the tennis courts who was wearing a fairly large cross. I had seen her at that table before, but this necklace was a recent development. I did a few more dives then went over to find out whether she might be of assistance.

"Hello," I said.

"Hello," she replied.

"You have a cross."

"Yes. I just bought this one."

I asked her what a good place might be to buy a cross.

"You could probably get one at the jewelry shop in the strip mall," she answered.

"Is that where you got yours?"

"No. This one is from a trip," she said. "My granddaughter was married last month. I have pretzels—would you like to sit down?"

"I can't necessarily stay," I said. "I'm swimming."

"You seem to be able to stay under water a long time."

"I'm working on that," I said. Assuming from the size of her pendant that she must frequent a church, or at least be an avid reader of the Bible, I asked her, "Do you know anything about heaven?"

"I guess that depends on what you mean by 'know.'" She put the bag of pretzels down between us. I told her I was in search of facts.

"Heaven facts are hard to come by," she said, "but I can tell you about my experience there."

I thanked her for the pretzels and suggested that perhaps the next day would offer an opportunity for us to speak again. I had not expected the offer of a personal nonfiction narrative rather than objective information and was happy to have extricated myself safely from the situation. I felt extremely lucky that my grandfather hadn't seen me talking to a stranger. It turned out, however, that he knew this woman. When I asked him in the elevator whether she was mentally ill and just functional enough to live in the condominium, he said that a long time ago she'd been a nun but that that didn't necessarily mean she was mentally ill. And he said she wasn't a nun anymore, so she must be feeling better.

The next day she was there again. I balked at first, but then, feeling as if I were being drawn against my will, I approached her table. Neither of us said anything, but she held out a small bag of mixed-together nuts, raisins, dried-up cranberries, and chocolate chips. I had never seen a snack like that before. "It's bridge mix," she said. "If the pretzels didn't harm you, this probably won't either." I extricated a raisin and took a seat. She asked about school, and I reminded her that it was now summer vacation. She said she had thought I might be enrolled in the vacation Bible school nearby.

"No," I said. "That would not be my parents' idea of a good summer for me." Then I asked her what she had meant by using the word *experience*.

"Only that facts are slippery," she said, "and cause a lot of fights. I say, if you can, stick to talking about things you know about from having gone through them." I asked her if she had gone through heaven. I remember making certain I had my flip-flops very much on in case it became time to go.

"Not all the way through it," she said, "but possibly into it—or something like it."

I recall deciding that it was important to get the subject on the table and asked whether her trip had occurred during her time spent as a nun.

"Did Bert tell you I was a nun?" The lady laughed. "Sometime tell him I was only a novice. The difference doesn't make much difference to folks in general, but it makes a lot of difference to nuns. You could say I didn't make it to nun."

I asked whether she had perhaps gone to her heaven-like setting in a dream. "Oh, no, I was awake," she said. "I was more awake than awake." And with that she began the story: her experience.

She told me that she'd been driving, using her community's car, on her way home from visiting family in another state. She was living in a convent at the time. "It had a library," she said, "a tiny one with bookshelves on every bit of wall, even above the doorframe. There was a book there of American art from the nineteenth century, and there was one picture I always went back to in it. It was a painting of a pale yellow shed on the side of a hill leading down to a river, with a fence trailing off out of the picture. For no reason at all, the first time I turned the page to that picture I heard my mind say, 'Oh, God's house.' After that I couldn't get it out of my mind that the yellow shed was God's house. I knew that would make all of heaven a small yellow shed, which was ridiculous, but I couldn't get it out of my mind. There was long grass and a pump. Whenever we prayed about heaven in the chapel, or the kingdom of heaven, I saw the yellow shed."

She said that she saw the shed from the highway as she was driving back; it was up ahead, the same shed. She told me she recognized it without question as the one from the picture—the one the artist must have sat in the field in front of, painting. She pulled off the road onto the dirt track that led up to it. "It was so beautiful I had to," she said. "I must have sat in the car for half an hour just looking at it, listening to cars whip along on the highway behind me. That's what I thought happened, anyway. The other driver said that while passing me she'd lost control of her sedan and had run me off the road.

"After about half an hour, as I said," she went on, "I knew I had to walk up the hill. Mostly I just knew I had to get out of the car, which had gotten terribly hot, but also something made me want to see inside the shed. The grass was dry and dead and quite high. The pump was stuck. Around the side of the building, the side the fence was on, there was a window, but I couldn't make out anything through it. So I forced the door open—I had to use my shoulder. I went in to get out of the heat more than anything. It was a dark little room full of mops, brooms, bleach, and floor wax, with shelves holding buckets and rags. A broom closet on a hill. I looked around then stepped back out the door. But the doorway, which should have deposited me back onto the hillside, didn't open onto the hillside. I wasn't looking out at the road—outside the room I was still indoors. What had been the shed was a closet in a big old country house. Not overly grand, I don't think, as grand homes go, but I couldn't tell; I couldn't get out of the servants' quarters.

"It took forever to find a door to the outdoors, but I did. I got into the kitchen garden. At the far edge of the garden, beyond a low stone wall, the land dropped away. I could see hundreds of stately homes, all of them built on wide terraces below me—down, down, down the side of a mountain. Which was a volcano. There were houses above, too. I passed through several of the houses but could never get into any of the grand rooms, only the kitchens, the pantries, places like that, rows of plain little bedrooms, then out again into the day.

"At last, a bit lower down," she said, "I came upon one of the houses full on, straight ahead. I could see the driveway leading through the main gate and directly up to the wide stairs and the official front door. I figured if I could get in the front door, I would finally be able to see some of the big, dignified spaces inside that the owners used. I knocked with the knocker to alert the staff, and a butler pulled the door open. He graciously invited me to step across the threshold into what he called the Great Hall. It was a room about ten feet square that seemed to be for hanging tools and drying the mud off boots. He welcomed me warmly, led me through a warren of hallways out into a yard, and introduced me to two other men, the gardener and gardener's assistant. I told them where I was from, and they asked all about the convent and politely told me their backgrounds as well. The butler said he'd been from York, in England, a

cooper. The gardener and his assistant said they'd been from
Sussex, where they'd been members of the international cel-
lular-phone sitcom sales-and-marketing police force. Then
the butler asked what I'd been told already about what he
called 'the position.' I didn't know what he meant and said
as much. He said he was sure we'd get it all sorted out, that
some people—especially those dazed by their recent experience with 'the light'—didn't understand about being servants right away. He said some people didn't understand for
quite a while, in fact.

"I asked about who owned the house, and whether there
was a schedule of tours for the public. He seemed baffled.
'Tours? What do you want to see?' he asked.

"'The big rooms. The pretty ones. The library, the ball-
room.'

"'Those rooms are in the part of the house where the
others live—the nobility, if you will. We're servants,' he said.
'We don't have access. We don't even have doors between.'

"'Then how do you serve them?' I asked.

"'We don't serve them—we serve each other,' he said.
'Most of us work in the house. These two take care of the
gardens, of course.'

"'They garden for each other?'

"'And for the rest of us. For themselves, as well. Having
a well-tended garden is pleasant for everyone. There's a man
for the horses. In the mornings I'm his valet, and then, after
seeing to them, he's mine. He's married to the cook. You'd
like her,' he added. 'She used to be from Latvia. She was a
cook.'

"'But what about the owners?'

"'I gather,' he said with a sigh, 'that the gentry don't have
much of a life.' I took that to mean that they had to serve
each other, and perhaps didn't know how. 'Oh, no, they certainly don't do that,' he stated vehemently. 'Once they
understand service, they turn up on our side.' Then with a
sigh he said, 'What's worse, until they understand, they're

scared stiff of the mountain, too—that it will explode and they'll cease to exist, that it will blow them and their precious personalities to ribbons.'

"'But you know it won't?'

"'I'm sure it will.'

"'It will?'

"'It's clearly not extinct. We get definite rumbles from time to time. I should say every now and again,' he corrected himself.

"'But you know you won't all cease to exist?'

"He took a long look up the slope, then an equally long one at me. 'It seems that in the step after this one, we're gone, however the second ending comes to each,' he said. 'And I don't think there's much chance that anything in the vicinity would survive an eruption—not body, not soul. Spirit, yes. Consciousness will remain,' he said. 'But not any that belongs to anyone in particular.' I asked him what the difference was if both groups knew they were going to be utterly terminated. 'We don't mind,' he said. 'They do.'

"We were all quiet for a while. As a conversational gambit, I think, the butler asked me how I'd enjoyed my 'life review.' I thought he was referring to a magazine. It turned out he expected me to have visualized all the events of my life simultaneously before I 'crawled out of the volcano.' I told him I hadn't crawled out of the volcano, seen my life, or been dazed by any bright lights, for that matter. I'd just stepped into one of the houses by accident, and out of it onto the mountain.

"'By accident indeed,' said the butler. 'Interesting. This hasn't happened in a while, not here, not with an adult. It used to happen all the time with Tibetans,' he added parenthetically, 'but most of them knew what they were doing.' The butler told me that back in the world I had come close to death, and was still close to it, but that my body hadn't quite died yet. Unlike the others who had come to reside on the mountain, I had a choice: I could stay in this world, ironing out the kinks caused by my unusual entry, or I could wrench myself back into that one. I asked whether, if I went back now, I could be sure of returning on the servants' side at the end of my natural life. He said no, I might enter on the owners' side, depending on my frame of mind at the time—or just as likely into any population of any of the many other available landscapes, about which he had no information. I reminded him that I was going to be a nun; he said that didn't count for much, unfortunately. I told him I would stay.

"'There's something to take into account before you decide,' he said, and he led me back into the house and along a passage to the doorway of a bedroom with a wide bed that had a small child asleep on it. 'You mean I'll have to be her nanny?' I asked. 'Until she grows into a servant too?' He explained that she was another who, like me, had arrived 'by accident' and thus had a choice about staying. Being a five-year-old, she had had no hesitation in saying she wanted to go home.

"I asked how long it had been since she'd come. He told me she'd arrived a month or so earlier. I said that was a long time for a child back on earth to be in a coma and suggested that her parents were probably inured to her loss by now. He explained that the span had been perceived as a month only in the world in which we were presently standing. That back in hers—hers and mine—the anesthesiologist involved in her surgery had probably seen her heartbeat falter just a second before and that her brain function was still intact. 'The materialist argument that with the death of the physical brain all mental processes must cease is—this may surprise you—both tenable and in fact correct,' he said, 'but the corollary, that at death each of us will perceive our own mental processes as ceasing, is based on an erroneous premise: that it takes more than the final split second's burst of brain activity to support a *perception* of continuity. Eternity, the ever-present Now, can be—indeed, is—experienced in

almost no time at all. Consider the mind's immediate fabri-
cation of a complex dream of several scenes created merely
in order to give a context—such as the signaling of an emergency in a firehouse—for an alarm clock's ring. That's why
it's so important how one greets death. Salvation and
damnation aren't eternal because Anyone wants them to be;
it's a matter of biochemistry. In a world mired in time there's
only enough time to establish one denouement.' It went
something like that. I put off thinking about it, I have to say;
we can talk about it later if you want to. The important
thing to the story is that he told me he'd like me to leave
and take her with me: she couldn't get back alone.

"I asked him why not. He said it had to do with the
nature of the trip. Silently, he took me to a part of the
grounds from which I could see straight up the mountain.
He pointed at a house made of steel and glass about two
hundred feet above us—terribly modern, lots of decks, lots
of levels, built right into the mountain itself. He told me one
terrace of that house had a pool and that the task was to
plunge to the bottom of the deep end, remove the cover of
the drain and swim down, right into the drain itself, possibly tugging oneself along its walls. I still didn't want to go,
but I could see why an adult was necessary. She'd never be
able to do that for herself. I asked whether the drain was big
enough to fit through.

"'No,' he said, 'but if it's going to work, you'll fit. Just get
into the pool and drag her into the drain as quickly as possible.'

"'Let's use the supply closet I came in through,' I suggested.

"'There are many ways in,' he said. 'This drain is the only
way out we know of.'

"'Why does it have to be so difficult?'

"'We don't know—we just know from reports that it
works. We have no idea how or why. You'll go?'

"I went. And that was that: we swam through the drain and back out into our lives." The woman leaned back, satisfied with her telling.

I asked how the woman had gotten the girl into the drain.

"We played for a while on the grass so she wouldn't be afraid of me, then the butler told her that she and I were to go swimming. She was happy to go; she said she had learned swimming that summer."

"But how did you get her through?"

"She slid right in."

"How did you get her down if she could swim?" I asked. "Wasn't she swimming up?"

"We both had to go down, to come back to this world."

I asked whether the woman had had to pull the girl underwater.

"I took her through the drain to help her. I brought her with me to save her, not to hurt her, honey."

"Was she screaming?" I asked. "With bubbles coming out? Was it hard to pull her through?"

"It was my job to bring her back. I was doing what I had been told to do."

"But what if it wasn't good to do, or it wasn't the way to do it? What if you were scaring her—or drowning her?"

"At that point in my life," said the woman, "I was learning obedience."

I saw she didn't know that the girl had lived.

"I'm sure she's alive," said the woman. "I fully believe she's alive."

"But it's not part of your experience."

"There are some things you can choose whether to believe," she said, "but there are some things you have to believe in order to keep on going."

HEAVEN ENOUGH

Addison Hall

Faith, like a jackal, feeds among the tombs, and even from
these dead doubts she gathers her most vital hope.
—Melville, *Moby Dick*

I CAME TO PEET'S for my morning coffee on a late
winter day; air mild, no sun. William and Mary were sitting
on the bench and I greeted them. "What happy chance
brings you here together on a weekday morning?" I said.
They stood up and came closer. "It's not so happy," Mary
said. "William's mother died last week, and we're just getting
ourselves organized."

I took in the story. His mother, unwell and eighty-one,
had a stroke and lingered for ten days, then died. One day
during the deathwatch, Mary was walking in town with
their eight-year-old son, Corson. William called from the
hospital, and Corson listened to Mary's side of the conversation. "Is she going to die?" he said, when Mary hung up.
"Yes," she said. He thought for a minute as they walked, then
he said, "It's not as if a child got lost in the snow. Children
are the future, but grandparents are the past."

Then he went on to ask about heaven, and with a pre-
cocity characteristic of him, delved into its problematics.
How could everyone get to do exactly what he or she

wanted in heaven, if doing it involved other people? How could the others do what one person wanted without compromising their own preferences?

Two currents ran under this conversation. One was our awareness that Mary is now almost completely recovered from a serious stroke of several years ago, a stroke that came out of the blue when she was in her mid-thirties. The other was our awareness that my own son John had died at twenty-five of colorectal cancer a year and a half ago. We didn't refer to either trauma, but I went away thinking about them, pierced by Corson's reference to the child lost in the snow.

Whenever a death occurs, those close to the dead one are left with a wound, a wound that heals faster if the dead one disappeared, like William's mother, in the normal sequence. When, like Corson's child in the snow, like John, the dead have disappeared out of sequence, the wound is slower to heal. Around the wound, bandages of improvised answers to persistent questions wind themselves. Heaven is one of those bandages, an ancient response to the need for meaning, for consolation, for some protection between the openness of the wound and the raw air of life going on.

"If there's a heaven," my wife said to John just before he died, "your grandfathers will be there to meet you." With the little energy he had left, John winked. He wasn't investing much in the prospect, however comforting it was meant to be. That wry refusal to be beguiled by false hope was true to his nature, and it is familiar to many of us, at least where the possibility of heaven is concerned.

I myself am more ambivalent about the possibility than ever. I know how deeply rooted, how universal, how resilient the impulse to claim heaven is. Not just when John died, but over and over in more than thirty years of work as

a priest, I've encountered grievers of intellectual sophistica-
tion, many of them agnostic at most, who in the aftermath
of the death of someone close have embraced the hope of
heaven with unembarrassed conviction. I've known countless others of straightforward faith for whom heaven is an
unquestioned assumption, especially but not only when
death strikes near them. Like others still, I am a skeptical
believer in heaven, one who would never defend the belief
if pressed, but who on the other hand embraces it, and will
be happy to embrace it until proven wrong, as I wouldn't be
surprised to be.

What I'm about to say in describing my beliefs about
heaven has no particular authority, except that of human
curiosity and imagination embroidered by the long tradition
of people—certain scriptural writers included—pondering
what comes next. To such a degree as my beliefs have been
strengthened by near-death experiences recounted to me
over the years by other people, I claim the persuasiveness of
their witness, and the remarkably coincident details of their
separate reports. Of course my hopes of heaven intensified
as John's death approached. Like mourners of the ages, rep-
resenting a wide range of religious traditions, I hope to be
with him again, and I hope that between now and then he
will be in the company of loving people, some of them
known to him before he died.

I believe in a heaven in which I will be reunited with
John and countless others, people whom I loved when they
were living and to whom I feel connected still. Though I
incline to introversion, I think of heaven as a social experience, one in which conversation and other group activities
can be engaged at complete leisure. In response to Corson's
anxiety, I would say that in heaven anyone's highest pleasure
is shared by his or her companions. Fleetingly in this life I
have known my own pleasure increased by abetting someone else's; in heaven I hope that rare earthbound altruism is
general, sustained, and beneficial to all concerned.

I believe, playfully and with no insistence that I could be right, that in heaven I will be able to meet and converse easily with the long dead and celebrated, who will welcome my interest in them. I imagine, for example, coming to the end of an animated conversation with Haydn and Mozart and sitting down with them at their urging to play through a little trio, one that we either know by heart or can improvise brilliantly *impromptu*. I hope to enjoy a session of this kind with Bob Dylan and Edith Piaf, their forlorn protagonists shining with a redemption of which their earthly originals were afraid, myself happily shifting back and forth from accordion to pedal steel.

Likewise I look forward to long innings of baseball, with ordinary people on the same teams and playing at the same level as some of my childhood heroes: Willie Mays, Sandy Koufax, Gil Hodges. I think what enjoyment I will have collaborating with Dame Edith Evans in a pickup performance of *The Importance of Being Earnest,* or sitting next to Mary Cassatt and Winston Churchill through a long gorgeous afternoon of landscape painting.

I imagine that there will be more exalted and explicitly holy experiences, and all of them stripped of what we know in this life as the anxious self-importance of religious pursuits. Pure joy and thankfulness, animated by constantly renewed energies of appreciation and delight, gathered up from time to time in a great chorus of praise; I imagine this under the supervision of Johann Sebastian himself.

Mostly I imagine that heaven is an experience suffused with love, a situation in which I receive all relationships as gifts of awesome worth, the humblest stranger being as precious to me as John or one of my exalted heroes. From the glimpses and sometimes sustained episodes that we receive in this life, we know how even the grimmest landscape and the worst weather and the most arduous exertion can be transformed and made beautiful when we are in the company of a person or of people whom we love and whose

love for us is certain. I imagine paradise to be an intensifica-
tion and broadening of that experience, a situation in which
we exchange love freely with other people, but (as Jesus
indicated) without the complications of physical desire and
possessive exclusiveness. Not only will we experience those
exchanges with other people, but also, to a greater degree
than we know in this life, we will give our love to God and
receive God's love for us.

Intimations of that life of sustained and utterly trustworthy love we receive already, both in dreams and in waking
life. We cultivate our hope of heaven, and assuage our impa-
tience for it, as we deepen our relationships to each other in
the present life. If in the end we die and disappear, and
heaven turns out to have been a harmless wish-dream, then
that deepening of loving relationships here will have to have
been heaven enough.

RUBIES THICK AS GRAVEL

Susan Wheeler

> ...And by the happy blissful way
> More peaceful pilgrims I shall see,
> That have shook off their gowns of clay
> And go apparelled fresh like me...
> Then the holy paths we'll travel,
> Strewed with rubies thick as gravel....
> > —"The Passionate Man's Pilgrimage,"
> > Walter Raleigh

> ...And curse Sir Walter Raleigh
> He was such a stupid get.
> > —"I'm So Tired," Lennon/McCartney,
> > lyrics by John Lennon

I WOULD LOVE (would I?) Sir Raleigh to be right: heaven as a swank spa, everyone in white robes, saints ladling nectar from crystal buckets, each step a step on a bed of rubies. But the reader in me says, *Wait*. Stop. Metaphor.

Two things that a priest in my home parish told me have come to me at least once a week in the intervening years. The first is that feeling is not faith, one of the first things bored pilgrims learn. This keeps me at prayer even when I sound like a sailor on Ritalin.

The second is an anecdote about Mother Teresa. Someone had asked Mother Teresa how she, seeing such suffering, could stay heartened and equal to the tasks before her. She replied (and I paraphrase a paraphrase) that she was replenished by prayer, and that regular prayer changed the quality of her attention. Instead of only taking in the suffering, through prayer she *noticed* the smallest acts of kindness and love—at times only brief blinks in the long days—and these sustained her. The fact that in misery and duress individuals were capable of such mercy sealed her faith in people as well as in the grace of God.

The first poem I came across that got close to my own idea of heaven was a poem by Ezra Pound called "'Blandula, Tenella, Vagula.'" The title, with its nonce "Tenella," was a take on the Emperor Hadrian's dying address to his soul, "Animula vagula blandula," or "O blithe little soul, flitting away." You'll see it's not that far from Raleigh's—although, three centuries later, its tone is more elevated.

> What hast thou, O my soul, with paradise?
> Will we not rather, when our freedom's won,
> Get us to some clear place wherein the sun
> Lets drift in on us through the olive leaves
> A liquid glory? If at Sirmio,
> My soul, I meet thee, when this life's outrun,
> Will we not find some headland consecrated
> By aery apostles of terrene delight,
> Will not our cult be founded on the waves,
> Clear sapphire, cobalt, cyanine,
> On triune azures, the impalpable
> Mirrors unstill of the eternal change?

Soul, if She meet us there, will any rumour
Of havens more high and courts desirable
Lure us beyond the cloudy peak of Riva?

I was eighteen, and had just decided that the best state in
which to be writing poems was akin to that of doing long-
division problems. Poetry—in its best sense—was like math,
I thought: clear, unclouded, absorbing, and coolly *blue,* the
counterpart to the heat of a liquid sun through olive leaves.
The "aery apostles" were "terrene" beside the poet and his
fellows "on the waves": in two lines, air, earth, and water.
That I didn't swim made the "cult...founded on the
waves" a little dangerous, a risk.

It is the sun that "lets" drift the liquid glory, but in that
word I saw the poet, too, *letting* in the sun. The movement
of the unstill mirrors—and the movement needed to ride
the waves—also had its counterpart in the receptivity of the
poet's tilt back, in his chair, face open, eyes closed, under the
overhang of olive branches in an Italian arbor. The intense
sun sifts in, infuses.

It was also a real place, a promontory Pound visited on
the southern shore of Lago dí Gardo, where Pound's favorite
Latin poet, Catullus, had taken refuge. In truth, Sirmio (now
Sirmione) is windy and changeable, with dramatic light and
cloud formations, mutable weather.

In the last year of her life, Simone Weil worked on a
"Statement of Human Obligation," her attempt at a universal moral law. The *attention* she called for was twofold. We
have in common, she argued, a core which is an "unques-
tionable desire for good," whether we are aware of this
desire or not, and then, around this core, our baggage, or
what she calls "an accretion of psychical and bodily matter."
We can only sustain awareness of this by "really directing the
attention beyond the world."

The reality of the world we live in is composed of variety. Unequal objects unequally solicit our attention. Certain people personally attract our attention, either through the hazard of circumstances or some chance affinity. For the lack of such ... other people remain unidentified. They escape our attention or, at the most, it only sees them as items of a collectivity. ... It is impossible to feel equal respect for things that are in fact unequal unless the respect is given to something that is identical in all of them. ... Anyone whose attention and love are really directed towards the reality outside the world recognizes at the same time that he is bound, both in public and private life, by the single permanent obligation to remedy ... the privations of soul and body which are liable to destroy or damage the earthly life of any human being whatsoever.

I am on a subway car. It's midafternoon, and a group of girls riding uptown hoot, shriek, call another group further down the car *bitches*. After school. Remember the angels on the subway in Wim Wenders's "Wings of Desire," before the movie took its turn toward schmaltz? A woman glances up from *Cosmopolitan,* reabsorbs. A boy sleeps against his mother's arm while she and her friend look at the girls disapprovingly. A man in dark green work clothes readjusts his haunches and stares at the floor. The angels would *notice* each, give each their attention, listen to their cores. Attention is a powerful antidote to inequality.

Simone Weil thought it was only through our attention to God that we could give our attention equally to all persons. But it may also be that through *noticing,* through a willed *attending to* those we would otherwise overlook, that we are able to get our glimpse of what is beyond this world. Some

poets launch right toward the unknowable. Some poets—
Elizabeth Bishop, one of them, said it also of her beloved
Gerard Manley Hopkins—"get to the spiritual through the
material." Some of us, of course, don't get off the ground.

Walt Whitman noticed.

> And the old drunkard staggering home
>   from the outhouse
> of the tavern whence he had lately risen,
> And the schoolmistress that passed on her way
>   to the school
> . . . and the friendly boys that passed
> . . . and the quarrelsome boys
> . . . and the tidy and freshcheeked girls
> . . . and the barefoot negro boy and girl,
> And all the changes of city and country
>   wherever he went.

"Greater than all the science and poems of the world,"
Whitman wrote, and "proved by its practical outcropping in
life, each case after its own concomitants," is "the intuitive
blending of love and faith in a human emotional character—blending for all, for the unlearn'd, the common, and
the poor."

Emerson said we make our own hell (and heaven—but
we're getting to that), and I do. I stop noticing. I see the
broad strokes, and they're terrifying. War, disaster, millions of
persons dying, suffering because of hubris or rigidity or dis-
interest, neglect. The flattener of a commerce that makes an
advertisement out of a work of art, out of a person; that fos-
ters hubris and neglect in its single purposed-ness. I extrap-

olate, assume; I get impatient with myself and everyone around me; I think the worst of us. My vision becomes foggy, cloudy, and my will clogged and obstinate. What I don't see, what I miss, is grace. I miss God.

John Bradford called it "this inferior region, where is nothing but travail and trials, and sorrow, and woe, and wretchedness, and sin, and trouble, and fear, and all deceiving and destroying vanities," but this was the whole of *life* for Bradford: "this comfortless race through this miserable earthly vale"; and perhaps he—in the Tower for sedition, soon to be put to death by burning—faced facts more squarely than I. This might be life and not hell—hell as beyond conception or description as heaven, as God. Endless estrangement from God, from clarity of vision or will— "abandon ye hope"—in whatever forms I can imagine, might bear no approximation to damnation at all.

I'm with Bishop. Whatever attempts I make to get at the spiritual proceed through the matter, in poems (even when that matter is the materiality of a nonce word). And even the triune azure of the waves changes, moves—one moment sapphire, the next cyanine; the experience of grace—the shifting dots of the sun's rays through the olive branches— shifts; the seeing, the apprehending, requires a supple eye. What for Raleigh was the sating of a thirst by nectar is, for me, the clear will that would make this eye supple—that, free of the residue of resistance or sludge of desire, would make me an open channel. A tilt back in my chair, a clear chute, a will open to God's direction: heaven.

For the rubies of mercy, when you know to look for them, are indeed thick as gravel.

Bibliographical Notes

Sir Walter Raleigh, "The Passionate Man's Pilgrimage," in *English Renaissance Poetry: A Collection of Shorter Poems from Skelton to Jonson,* second edition, ed. John Williams (Fayetteville: The University of Arkansas Press, 1990), 152–153.

John Lennon and Paul McCartney, "I'm So Tired," from *The White Album,* lyrics by John Lennon.

Ezra Pound, "'Blandula, Tenella, Vagula,'" in *Personae of Ezra Pound* (New York: New Directions Books, 1971), 39. Copyright 1926 by Ezra Pound. Reprinted by permission of New Directions Publishing Corp.

Simone Weil, *Two Moral Essays: Draft for a Statement of Human Obligation* (Wallingford, Penn.: Pendle Hill Publications, 2006).

Walt Whitman, "Leaves of Grass" and "November Boughs," in *Walt Whitman: Complete Poetry and Collected Prose* (New York: The Library of America, 1982), 138, 1243.

"I TELL YOU A FURTHER MYSTERY"

Alan Jones

HEAVEN. WHAT AN impossible subject! I made the mistake of "Googling" the word "heaven" and found plenty of websites with lots of information and details about heaven as the place you go to (if you're lucky) when you die. I've noticed too that thoughts of heaven can bring out our vindictive side. One of the joys of heaven is to be able to relish the punishments of those in the other place. There's a nasty side to it all.

Christians inherit two basic views of heaven. The popular Western version tends to be of the static angels-and-harps variety. I prefer the Eastern version. It has more of the flavor of dynamic continuity. We move "from glory to glory" right now, not simply after we're dead. In the Eastern tradition, human beings long for the infinite. We are not fixed entities, but beings-in-process, defined by an infinite longing which pulls the soul forward in an infinite progression. We live out the questions, and it might take longer than a lifetime.

Music might be a good place to start. The harmony and counterpoint of my life-in-communion (at least at those precious moments when things come together) teach me about heaven, because they teach me about beauty.

I remember with gratitude and affection my training in England as a choir boy in a great tradition of choral music. It changed and shaped my life. I am convinced that the music influenced the way I approach and think about theology—in poetic and metaphorical terms. Each of us, perhaps, possesses a piece of music that speaks to us more deeply than any words. Some time ago I discovered the *Incarnatus* from one of Palestrina's masses—fifty seconds of music that deepen and strengthen my faith. Music like this speaks of three basic human experiences: thoughts about death, the desire for happiness, and the reality of love. We learn, sometimes painfully, that "here we have no abiding city." Appreciation of our own instability causes us to reevaluate what really matters. Music can be the point of entry into the kind of vulnerability that opens the heart and teaches it to trust.

Great music contributes to the recovery of something we sorely need: *piety.* At the heart of piety is the glory of helping to make the world a welcoming and hospitable place. When I lose myself in a creative activity, when I delight or am distressed by art—not just by music, but art in all its forms—I get a glimpse of the world as God wills it. This is an act of piety. And conversely, every time I share in the Eucharist, I sense its symphonic quality. For Christians, the best metaphor for heaven is a banquet. Heaven is not a place you go to when you die. Heaven is present now, all around us, a code word for where God is—in the music, in the feast.

So the question of heaven isn't an intellectual puzzle which *in principle* has an answer. If there is life after death it begins *now.* At the moment, I find myself occupied by the question "Is there life after birth?" So, whatever heaven is, it isn't about "the hereafter." The danger of imagining heaven as a destination or a final resting place is that we miss the glory of the present. To quote the wise theologian N. T. Wright, if heaven is going some place it's "going to be with

God in the place where he has been all along." It's about presence or, better, Presence right now.

My adventure into fullness of life (which I take to be the kingdom of heaven) involves reading, writing, and great conversation—preferably over a good meal. It is nourished by the arts, especially music. But there is a paradox here, one that the mystics might understand. What are virtues for the mystics are torments for many of us: alienation, loneliness, silence, solitude, interior emptiness, stripping bare, poverty, not-knowing, *emptiness*. The arts have, more often than not, given me an experience of being emptied. What we really need is often to be found in what we dread most—risk, not being in control, in the emptiness of the self. This doesn't sound much like "heaven," but how else can we make an inner space for living with ourselves and with each other? Cultivating gratitude helps us draw out the gold that is often hidden in the loneliness, the silence, the interior emptiness, the suffering, the poverty, and "the knowledge-that-knows-nothing."

Emptiness, then, is indispensable to true enjoyment of the world because true enjoyment has nothing to do with *possession*. It is the kind of emptiness that encourages me to give myself away to others in love and service. Heaven isn't a private possession, anymore than music, anymore than food.

Food is a delight. I love cookbooks and miss the times when the whole family would gather together to make bread. There was flour all over the kitchen and we loved to throw the dough around—especially the smooth oily dough of challah. There's no pleasure quite like preparing and cooking a meal with the bounty of the earth. Where is the food for the soul? It is in the "useless" activities of music and play. We get a taste of heaven in the various ways in which we "waste" our time eating and drinking and delighting in one another.

The Reverend William Archibald Spooner, dean and later warden of New College, Oxford, suffered from *metathesis*—a speech defect concerning the transposition of words and syllables. In one sermon he is supposed to have said, "We all know what it is to have a half-warmed fish inside us." This spoonerism combines the pleasure of what it is to have a good meal (a half-warmed fish inside us) and what it is to be full of hope and longing (the half-formed wishes of the human heart). Our lives are punctuated by half-formed wishes, with longings and aspirations we cannot quite put into words.

Life can be seen as a cycle of feasting and fasting—a seesaw between necessity and delight. A shared meal is one place where joy easily finds a place—from a starving child grateful for a crust of bread to a wedding banquet for a prince and princess. It's not surprising that, over the centuries, there developed elaborate laws of hospitality and etiquette. It has something to do with the fact that we are both hosts and guests on the earth. Sometimes we play one role, sometimes another. Most of us know what it is to serve a meal to others and to have one served to us. We also know that there is something truly vile about being betrayed by someone with whom one has shared table fellowship. This vision of a banquet is also intensely political, because the meal we share is for everyone. In the heavenly vision, no one is turned away from the table. Thus, "heaven" is experienced when time slows down enough for us to enjoy each other and be truly present to one another. And a banquet is just the place. *"Pâté de foie gras* to the sound of trumpets": that comment by an exuberant nineteenth-century cleric sets the right tone. Heaven, whatever it is, sharpens the senses. Whatever we *really* enjoy in this life is a glimpse of life in all its fullness. It's somehow an anticipation of heaven.

I cannot eat certain foods without being taken back to certain places. One whiff of rosemary and I am cooking lamb for twenty in New York thirty years ago. The smell of roasted peppers takes me back to a friend who first taught me to roast them in the oven and then steam them in a paper bag before peeling them. I still remember our delight in each other's company as we covered the peeled peppers with garlic and olive oil. There are other foods that remind me of certain rituals when the children were growing up. I cannot eat a pancake (or more accurately a crepe) without thinking of the Saturday morning ritual with my children when they were little. Saturday meant pancakes. And not any old kind of pancakes. English pancakes with sugar and lemon juice, not the flapjacky kind with blueberries and syrup. All of us could play this game with various foods. Food is often the gateway to memory. And memory and hope are the ingredients of heaven.

When I think of food, I also think of the houses in which my heart once lived. Heaven is like coming home because "home" is where they have to take you in (or, at least, they are supposed to) no matter what. Being "at home" with ourselves doesn't seem that common, but we cannot live the truth of who we are if we aren't familiar with the citadel of ourselves and know what is inside. St. Teresa of Avila warns us that many of us are so uncomfortable with ourselves that we cannot feel at home with what is inside us. That's hell. We lurk in the outer courtyard of our hearts, too frightened to come in.

We all want an invitation to the banquet of life, a place at the table. There is something isolatingly terrible about not being welcome—like poor kids sticking their faces right up against the window to watch the people feasting inside. Like Oliver Twist daring to ask for more. Yet some of us find ourselves at a feast when we would rather be somewhere else— like Alice caught up at the Mad Hatter's tea party. Alice asks the Cheshire Cat a fundamental question: "Would you tell me, please, which way I ought to go from here?" Will we end up at a place of welcome? Will there be room at the table? Will there be enough food to go around? A relaxing meal with people we trust is one of the antidotes to the madness of the world. But at the Mad Hatter's tea party you weren't allowed to sit still for long. When you have to eat with March Hares, the best thing to do is to put your head down, eat as fast as possible, and escape at the earliest opportunity! A *shared meal* is one of the ways in which the saints understood heaven. In fact, reality is by definition something shared. A purely private reality would be hell. Sharing is a natural consequence of seeing the world as it really is. Being is communion.

Terrence Rattigan wrote a play many years ago that was made into a movie. *Separate Tables* is about people—sad, pathetic, isolated—living in a pretentious and slightly run-down seaside hotel where the dining room was proud to offer the clientele the amenity of eating at separate tables. The movie is about the breakdown of that system, which mirrored the actual existence of the guests. True security is to be found in social solidarity rather than in isolated individual effort. The terrible individualism of "separate tables" came to an end when some of the guests saw how unnaturally they were separated from one another.

This is the human quandary: the more the individual grows aware of his or her distinctiveness, the greater the isolation. That's why we clutch after each other with a gnawing need and call it love. We are destined to disappoint one another. Our loving often leads to a nightmare of anxiety. This is why the holidays or parties or vacations can be such a pain and disappointment. They cannot deliver what they promise. You can't talk about heaven without talking about hell.

Here's my final shot at getting at the subject. It was a sunny afternoon in Paris a few years ago. I took the Metro to Montmartre and walked up the steps to Sacré-Coeur when all of a sudden the world was ablaze with glory and the light of it was around me and in me and shining through everything. Sheer joy. Where did this joy come from, with

its gift of presence and rightness? What triggered it? Was it
the kid with the ice cream—great gobs of it dripping down
her seraphic face? Was it the couple who had eyes only for
each other, entwined in wonder on the grass? Was it the
sunlight playing on the leaves of the trees, delighting the eye
with every shade of green imaginable? I don't know and I
could drive myself crazy trying to work it out. All I do know
is that it had something to do with God, that God was in it
and that God was the cause of it.

Joy is a bit like reading a story that never comes to an
end. You get caught up in it, even lost in it. The joy of it is
that it is all gift. God gazes at us from every human face,
because all are brothers and sisters of the divine. Joy has
something to do with sight, with seeing God in all people,
and when we aren't available to the surprise we miss the
point of our existence to play host and guest to each other.

Joy is strange because there are sometimes tears mixed up
in it. Not always but sometimes. God is seen in the hungry
or angelic face of a child, in the hopeful, resigned, or resent-
ful faces of the poor, in the strained features of someone
who has begun to face up to the consequences of its own
sinning. God is seen even in the faces of those we fear and
hate, and looks back at us through their eyes. And those eyes
reflect love in both its merciful and angry aspects. You never
know when God is going to surprise you—and stun you
with a joy that makes your eyes wet with tears.

Joy in this fuller aspect widens and deepens our range of
anticipation of what it might mean to be human. It points
to our true end as persons. The process brings with it an
ever-greater wealth in the forms of individuality that can be
minted. Ever richer forms of social relationship develop. No
two snowflakes are exactly alike, and a human being—a
being with a history—cannot be cloned. Joy—unrepeatable
and uncontrollable.

At the end of Dorothy L. Sayers's *Gaudy Night* Lord Peter
Wimsey says to Harriet: "I have nothing much in the way of

religion, or even morality, but I do recognize a code of behavior of sorts. I do know that the worst sin—perhaps the only sin—passion can commit, is to be joyless. It must lie down with laughter or make its bed in hell—there is no middle way."

Joy is silence and adoration and becomes our *raison d'être*. Adoration isn't stupefaction in the face of an all-consuming divinity. Adoration is the amazement at being our true selves in the Divine Presence. Joy makes adoration, compassion, and community possible. And while these are possible, so are we. But I mustn't forget the kid with the ice cream, the lovers in the park, and all those greens of the leaves that luminescent afternoon on Montmartre.

HER LAST HOURS
Nora Gallagher

THREE WEEKS AFTER my mother died, I dreamed that I lived in a house with the tape of a dog barking in the basement. The dog barked on and on. Sometimes it muttered and howled. For my husband and me, it was the background of our days, a constant noise we had grown accustomed to and had to live with. Then, one day, in the dream, it stopped.

My mother, Julie Walcott Gallagher, was a month away from her eighty-ninth birthday when she died in a hospice in Las Cruces, New Mexico, in early 2006. My father, David, had died five years before, in October 2001, a month after the towers collapsed on 9/11.

She was the daughter of a Chicago architect—my grandfather designed houses and public buildings, among them an English gothic Episcopal church along the north shore of Lake Michigan—and she inherited his talent for design and rendering. Entirely self-taught, she built one beautiful adobe house after another in New Mexico where I grew up. One of my earliest memories is of watching her at the dining room table working with pencil and graph paper. And when she died, the images that came to me were architectural: moving from one room to another, crossing over a threshold, inhabiting a room far different from every other: *In my Father's house are many mansions.*

She was a wonderful companion for a child. She and I used to reenact the scene in *The Wind in the Willows* when Rat and Mole, lost in the forest, find Badger's boot scraper under the snow. We lived in Aspen, Colorado, at the time, and we would bundle up, go outside, and pretend that we had lost our way.

"Oh, Mole," she would say to me, "I think I've felt something!" And I would walk over to her, and take her hand, and together we would dig and pretend that we'd found Badger's front door and our way to safety.

In the same way that she designed and built our houses, she built an emotional dwelling place as well, as surely as she made a room or a wall. And that place was at once dreamy and filled with light and charm, stories and pretending, and then, as if overnight, cold with rage and brooding. Her personality was present in the rooms she built, and present in the lives of her family. It was nearly impossible to get away from her—all of her—the charm, the wit, the energy, and then, the volatile temper, the brooding depression, the league of resentments.

Someone asked me once what my most symbolic memory of my mother was and I replied it was the locked bedroom door, behind which she lay on the bed, waiting for someone, one of her children or her husband, to knock and apologize. We always did, fearing that her threat—I won't come out—meant forever.

My husband once said that loving my mother was like putting a spoon down a garbage disposal: you had to brace yourself. A spoon in a garbage disposal, a barking dog.

Because we did not know, as children, that she was in some kind of serious trouble—she may have had a personality disorder (this, too, like her skill at design, passed from generation to generation)—we explained it to ourselves the way children always do: it was normal to walk on eggshells around one's mother and if something went wrong, we were to blame. She loved younger children and dogs; what she loved were things that could not separate from her. Her grandson, my nephew Sean, became the thing she loved most of all.

She lived for her last five years in a small compound—a sunny house with a one-room guest house across a graveled courtyard. Sean lived in the guest house. In his early twenties, Sean was diagnosed with schizoid-affective disorder, and from then on, my mother insisted on taking care of him. Every time someone in the family intervened and separated them, my mother found a way to bring him back home.

In 2000, my mother complained of a lump on her jaw for a few too many months and I persuaded her to come to California to be checked out. The surgeon at UCLA took about ten minutes to diagnose lymphoma. For the next nine months, she lived around the corner from my husband and me, across the street from the cancer center. She never went out of her hotel room except to the doctor. She came to our house only once. Yet, I liked taking care of her. I found her once in the middle of an almost empty hospital, late at night, after she'd had an MRI and I'd gone out to get her medications. She was an old woman standing alone in a corridor and as I rushed toward her, her whole face lit up.

My father, who was 88, was left alone with Sean in Las Cruces. He called one day and told me he had fallen in the supermarket parking lot. I traveled back there to check on them and found my father and Sean living like two old men in a boarding house: Sean making coffee in the morning spreading the grounds like black seeds all over the counters; my father washing his pajamas and sheets every day because he had drenched them in sweat in the night. In those days together, he told me something of his life with my mother. He loved her, and he knew her, and he spoke to me as truthfully as he had ever spoken in his life. One night he said, "I don't think she is capable of intimacy."

Dad wanted to move to Santa Barbara, joining my
mother there, and place Sean in a clinic and halfway house
in Albuquerque. My father was so afraid of my mother that
he tried to foist the whole plan off on me, but I insisted he
consult with her every step of the way. She couldn't stop us,
and she knew it. I would find out, later, how angry and
insulted she felt. In one monster snowstorm in January
2001, my husband moved my father, the household possessions, and the cat to Santa Barbara, and I moved Sean to
Albuquerque.

For six months, we had what I thought was an uneasy
settling in, and then, at lunch one day, my mother
announced that she and my father were moving back to Las
Cruces. They moved in June and four months later my
father died. A month after that, during Thanksgiving week,
I called the halfway house to talk to Sean and they told me
he had walked out the door. My mother had sent him a
one-way bus ticket.

From then on, my mother refused to see me. From 2001
to a few days before her death, she equivocated, elaborated,
ducked, and covered, but the message was the same. I would
half-heartedly say, I'd like to come see you, and she would
say, I have a toothache, it's not a great time. Or, I am so tired,
another time. Or, you can't come because of "what happened with Sean."

She and Sean lived together in a state all too easy to
imagine although, God knows, I probably don't have it
right. He sat in his guest house playing the guitar, smoking
weed, and talking to his voices: one day he was a Dominican
monk and the next the King of France.

She made notations on her daily calendar. "Talked to S.
about marijuana."

A cleaning person and caregiver came in twice a week.
The cabinets were full of Captain Crunch cereal and chocolate bars. When I went over to the house the day after she

died, there was a half-eaten bowl of cereal in the basket of
her walker beside her bed.

By the fall of 2005, she was going blind from macular
degeneration and had a recurrence of lymphoma. "I don't
want chemotherapy," she said.

"I understand," I said. Her voice was strung up tight and
high. Her doctor put her on steroids and painkillers. In a few
more days, she was euphoric. The steroids had given her
extra energy and the painkillers made her stoned. She survived for a few more months that way.

But in early January, I called and she answered sounding
as exhausted as I have ever heard a person, her voice rasp-
ing, her breath coming slow and hard. She was going into
the hospital that night, her therapist was taking her. She had
withheld from me all of the names of the people who knew
her, but she gave them all to me that night. I told her she
would be fine, and she said, "Tell me that again."

Her therapist called me late that night and said she was
better, she had only been dehydrated. But the next day the
nurse said she had failed the swallow test and was having
trouble speaking. I made reservations for Vincent and me to
fly out the next morning. Sean's brother, my nephew
Robert, and his wife Michele made plans to leave in a few
days.

From Denver, I called the hospital to ask the nurse to tell
my mother I was coming. When we arrived in El Paso, I
checked in with Robert, who told me that my mother had
thrown a fit when she found out I was on the way. She told
the nurse to call me back and tell me not to come. (And the
nurse, a brave woman, told my mother she would not obey
her. "She's your daughter," she said to her. "She needs to be
here.") I drove to Las Cruces in a furious, frantic rage. And
when we got to the hotel, I prayed and the thought came to
me that it wouldn't go as I liked. It never does.

When I arrived, that first night, after the nurse told me
she was finally asleep, I peered around the corner of the

door. I saw the sleeping face of a witch. Her head was thrown back, the cords in her neck were standing out like strings. Her expression was screwed down to fear and rage. I blew her a kiss and left. The next day her oncologist told her I was there and wanted to see her, and she whispered, "Tomorrow." Such was my state that I viewed this as good news.

That evening, I made myself go into her room. She was sleeping or dozing. I took her hand. She opened her eyes. My heart froze. She looked at me, probably not being able to see my full face, and made the sound "Nor, Nor," as if to say, I hoped, Nora. But it might have been "No." Then she slept.

I sat with her on Monday while they prepared the papers for her to go into hospice. She dozed, and held my hand. I thought, this may be all I get.

On Tuesday morning we moved her in an ambulance to the hospice, La Posada, a low building on the far side of town from the hospital. We came in through a back entrance and as we entered, I felt the peace of the place. It made the hospital feel like an airport.

Her room was large. It had a hospital bed, a comfy lounge chair upholstered in blue velour, and a view of a tree and a small garden. The nurse told us they were working on getting a morphine prescription from her doctor, and Adavan, a tranquilizer. They hooked up oxygen for her, but the nurse said it probably wasn't doing much good. He told me they didn't suction there, so I feared she would choke to death, but when we lifted the head of the bed, she seemed to breathe more easily. She kept brushing at the mask, and I finally took it off.

At first she was agitated. She moaned and held her stomach. I worried that she was in pain, badgered the nurse to hurry the medicines, paced the hall. Gradually, however, she quieted down and, at the same time, woke up. Whatever drugs they were giving her in the hospital must have worn off.

She began to look around. Her face relaxed. The lines were gone. She could not speak, but she could make little noises and move her mouth.

I was sitting in the chair across the room while Vincent leaned over her, sponging her lips with one of those little square hospital sponges on a stick like a lollipop. She was closely watching him.

Then she lifted her hand—I watched her do this—and placed it flirtatiously on his sleeve. It was as if she were asking him to dance. And then my husband said, "Oh, Judy, aren't you something."

Then he said, "Nora is here." And then, to me, "You'd better come over here. She's looking excited."

I walked over to the bed and leaned over her. She looked up at me, and turned her head to see me out of the periphery of her eye. And then she took my hand and placed it on her heart. It was a gesture of intimacy that she had never managed in her long, barking dog's life. I, who had worked my way to a wary distance from her, could hardly believe it was happening. She held my hand against her chest and I left it there. Under my hand I felt her old skin, thin as paper, and under that, her faintly beating heart. Then she lifted her hand and placed it over mine. Her palm covered me like the shelter I had longed for all my life.

Then, slowly, with great care, she took my hand in hers, and moved it to her face. She placed my palm against her cheek, and moved it up and down, up and down, a little smile playing at the corners of her lips. I looked into her nearly blind eyes, and she turned her face to see me better. We did that give and take you do with babies, the peering into the eyes, the little smile, the returning look. We allowed each other in at last.

We spent the afternoon like that, the three of us. Vincent and I changed places at her bedside. We sponged her mouth.

I watched her eyes. I held her hand. Her face was smooth.
Her eyes were like the eyes of a child or a delicate bird. A
creature. Curious, delighted. She was, we were, there is no
other word for it, changed.

How is it that things fall away? The hours of that afternoon
were like a wave set off by a stone dropping into a pool of
water; the ripples reverberated backward through her life.
The past is not what we think it is. It is not written in stone
after all, but can be washed over and through by the present's
events.

I felt I understood a part of the resurrection. Jesus rode a
wave backward into time and human history and redeemed
events, that is, stole them back from chaos and destruction.
He walked among the dead and woke them up with the
power of the same thing that stood with us that afternoon.
In the mind of God, there is no past or present and nothing
ever dies.

I felt freed from the past. Not from the memory of the
past, not from the historical record, but from its tyranny over
my present life. What had been closed down by the past's
influence was freed to wander: a new pattern of events was
set free in me. Right away, I saw my mother's life as if from
a different window. Right away, I said to myself, not "she
tortured me," but "she led a tortured life." And, in the days
to come, I "recovered" memories, not only of trauma, but of
other times, like the way we found our way in the snow to
Badger's door and safety.

That afternoon, whatever we had done together in our
lives, or failed to do, the fragments of love in all three of us
were gathered up so that they coalesced to the point of profound connection. We crossed over, my mother leading the
way. It was as if a door had opened into heaven, allowing
heaven in. *In my Father's house are many mansions.* It matters

that it was only a fraction of a long life, a few hours at the end of eighty-eight years, but it was, for then, and for now, enough.

In the hospice, it was early evening, my mother's favorite time of day. Robert had called to say his plane had landed and he was on his way. I had lifted the shades and my mother was looking out at the tree in the garden. Vincent and her caregiver were standing by the bed, talking. Her breathing slowed. I told them. And then it stopped. A nurse came and took her pulse, and said she had "passed." I was shocked. I had never seen a person die so quickly. Then, after minutes, I swear it, she took a breath and began again. And as Robert walked in the door, crossed the room, and took her hand, she stopped for good.

THEN IT'S JUST THE FIREWORKS

The Monks of Mariya uMama weThemba Monastery

THE FOUR OF US are sitting together in the library of the small house that currently serves as our living quarters in Grahamstown, South Africa. We are preparing to move into the new monastery building next door, so the room is something of a mess. The table where we sit is covered with drawing plans, paint swatches, fabric samples, furniture brochures, report cards from children sponsored by our scholarship fund, letters requesting other assistance and other papers, plastic mailboxes filled to the brim. Another table stands nearby, piled high with newspapers and periodicals. A dog lies sleeping at our feet and a dying fire hisses in the fireplace. The Eastern Cape sunlight streams through dusty windows. The sound of hammering, electronic saws, and workers' voices fills the room as we try to conduct our discussion. We are imagining heaven in the midst of a construction site.

You would think, given the circumstances, that we might want to imagine heaven being as far away as possible from all this daily chaos. But in fact, we have some difficulty imagining heaven as someplace else. That's the strange thing about monks, particularly Benedictines. If we attempt to think about it at all, we imagine heaven right where we are. In all the tumult of this building project, as we seek to push deeper roots into the South African earth, we are being true to our vows, as St. Benedict proclaimed them twelve centuries ago: obedience, stability, and conversion of life. These vows have everything to do with the here-and-now: the monastic imagination has this grounded quality.

In talking about heaven the way we do, we're also being true to the way Benedictines tend always to discuss important matters—as a community. We are three Americans and one Namibian, living in one of the most beautiful and most impoverished rural areas in the Eastern Cape. The four of us are different ages and at various stages in our monastic vocation. Timothy, our prior, has been a monk the longest, over twenty-five years. Andrew comes next in seniority, and then John. Daniel has been a monk for only about ten months. But in a Benedictine community, we all have equal voice. As Benedict says in his Rule, great wisdom is just as likely to come from the mouth of the newest member as from that of the most senior. Our wisdom grows from listening to each other.

What we said in this conversation surprised us. Given the demands of living in the here-and-now, we don't usually have time to talk about such matters as heaven and the afterlife. We had never really told each other what we thought about these things. The most welcome surprise was that, with all the differences among us in age and length of service, our conversation came to a graced convergence in the end, even if we didn't come near to exhausting heaven's possibilities. As Timothy remarked, "We're all pretty much on the same track, wherever that's going." So here is the conversation we had.

Timothy: I don't give much thought to what heaven is and I don't find much evidence in the Rule that it was much of a concern to Benedict, either. He does say in the seventy-second chapter, "May Christ lead us into everlasting life." But there is no kind of Book of Revelation–style vision of heaven. In the opening sentence of the Rule, Benedict calls seekers into the community by inviting us to listen for the presence of God right now among us. Listening "with the ear of the heart" allows love to grow within us. And then there is Benedict's emphasis on Christ: finding Christ and living in Christ. We begin with listening carefully, and what we hear is an invitation into the "school of the Lord's service"—the service and recognition of Christ in all of creation, in all that is. Any person who comes to the monastery is to be received as Christ. What we are earnestly running toward and seeking is the presence of Christ *now.*

Gregory the Great remarked that Benedict saw the whole of creation in a single ray of light. I think of this as a prism. Light is broken down into a lot of different colors, all part of that single ray of light. For me Christ is the prism. As the light shines through Christ, we then see all the individual lights that make up that single ray. Each one of us in community is like one of those broken-up pieces of individual light; each one of us has our own hue, our own shade, our own wonderful color, our own personality. If all of us have loving respect for the abbot, fear of God, and love and respect for each one of the brothers, Christ then leads us back through his prismatic self, if you will, to the Father, to God Who Is. That's the way I understand a Benedictine monastic community and for me, that's reality in God.

Andrew: I don't wake up in the morning and think, "One day we're going to be in heaven." But I do remember that when I was a youngster, heaven was really important because I was going to see loved ones again. There's a reunion. And then I got more cynical and more educated.

But that thought came back to me when we heard the other morning that one of our brothers, Douglas, had died suddenly in the States. Heaven has to do with community as well, a community beyond time and place. I still believe in the reality of the hope that heaven is not just our disappearing into the Great Spirit. Scripture and Benedict imply that heaven is something we look forward to.

John: Benedict's Rule is a re-doing of the earlier, anonymous *Rule of the Master,* which is always looking forward to heaven. Benedict removed a lot of that language, and talks instead about what's going on here on earth rather than what's going to happen in the future. But Andrew, I liked what you said about community beyond time and place. Maybe right now we are practicing for the endless alleluias, as our founder, James Huntington, liked to say. Often when I try to imagine heaven I get a blank. But when I think of living the community life, Timothy's image of the prism reminds me of the prayer we say at the end of the Eucharist every day. We say we are all members of that one body, or as you put it, Timothy, we are all pieces of that one light. I can see a vision of being around a eucharistic table in heaven, and of course that's what we're doing now in having this conversation.

Daniel: When I grew up it was either/or, heaven or hell. And everything you did was in order not to go to hell. Never mind what heaven was. I still don't have a clue what heaven was growing up. All I knew, I was scared of hell. And as I grew older and as I became more cynical, and more disillusioned with what was happening in my country, and I guess became more disillusioned with God, whatever image of heaven I might have had just disappeared. Then through all the years, as I kept on with my struggle with God, I was attracted to monasticism. Now that I find myself continually progressing in my monastic journey, I still don't give a lot of thought to heaven, because I am still not comfortable with its being an alternative to hell. I don't even have a concept of what hell is. But if I have to imagine heaven, it would be in a moment of knowing God, of meeting God. Whether it's here or in the hereafter, I don't know. Heaven, if it has to be anything, will be part of the mystery of God. So I don't really even know how to imagine that.

Timothy: I think of what Paul says. Absolutely nothing can separate us from the love of God in Christ Jesus. When I was a child, I would look up at all the stars and would think, "Oh wow! When I die I will get to go to all of those stars at the exact same moment." And that was . . . heaven. It's a great comfort knowing that I don't have to be perfect because Paul has already said, nothing is going to separate me. What I hear in Benedict is that our living in the light of that joy is what causes the kingdom to erupt in this place, in this time, when we're living in the light of the resurrection. The second coming of Jesus will happen, but it will happen for a community; it doesn't happen for just one individual. We get the image of hell, or sin, or whatever you want to call it, when we lose that perspective.

Andrew: I've spent a lot of time with death working in the hospital. And I have had a lot of time to observe what people are like when they die or what the families are like. The consistent theme is always hope in the end. That is the way people find comfort. And I think that's the difference between a Christian concept of heaven and something else. Every religion has some concept of heaven where the good get to go or the heroes get to go. It seems that what we hear from scripture and what we experience is that anyone who wants to go, goes. The only thing that separates me from heaven is me. And I *can* separate myself. That option is there. But if I do not want to separate myself, then I cannot defeat God. I read in the psalms that your life is seventy years and

if you're really lucky and hit the lotto it is eighty. I am coming up on sixty-nine, so heaven is a wee bit more important
for me than for someone at thirty. But I have a feeling that
as a Christian, all the relationships that I have that are unfin-
ished, all the relationships that are pained, will be wrapped
in the love of God, in that light. I don't think my idea of
heaven is sentimental. My idea of heaven is the culmination
of the hope of God. If there is no heaven, I won't feel
cheated.

Daniel: Because you won't know.

Andrew: Well, even if I do know, being in Christ now, knowing God now is enough. Heaven is the bonus. "You say that
if you had brought us through the Red Sea, it would have
been enough." So heaven is more than enough.

Daniel: But if you believe in God, you believe in the hereafter and everlasting life. We pray it so often. We listen to that
being said and sung. So there has to be something. That is
the question. What is that something? I really don't know.

Timothy: That's why I can't talk about it. If we had the most
learned theologian in the world sitting in this room, he or
she would still be speculating. As both Paul and John say, no
one's ever seen God. But John *does* say that we have seen
each other. And if we love each other then we've seen God.
It can be avoiding the realities, spending one's time project-
ing out what heaven is going to be like. That's navel-gazing.
We can do that for our entire lives and we'll still never
know.

Andrew: My New Testament professor used to say that what
a Christian has to do is bet his life on God. There's no guarantee. But you go ahead and live that love anyway.

Daniel: What's the use of faith if you know that there's going to be a reward?

Andrew: But it's not possible without hope.

Daniel: No, it's got to be grounded in something. Otherwise it's fatalistic.

Timothy: And what Paul says is that faith and hope are grounded in love. That's wonderful. We have faith, we have hope, and we have love, and he says that the greatest of these is love because love is faith and hope in action. Love is an act. Love is not a sentiment of heart. And faith and hope are possible in the action of love.

John: How Benedict describes it is the inexpressible delight of love. You can't really talk about love.

Timothy: You can only act it.

John: And then, the kingdom breaks in. Or we see it. It's always there, but we suddenly have a clear vision of it.

Daniel: An awareness. But come back to the theme of the whole conversation, imagining heaven: it's the ultimate conspiracy theory. By no means do I mean that heaven is a figment of the imagination. But you can imagine heaven in any way you want to and no one can contradict you. Nobody has got the facts and those who do won't give them to you. That's the fun about heaven, I suppose, that eventually you can do anything you want to with it.

Timothy: And that's the challenge of Jesus, because Jesus doesn't fire off into the ozone in his ministry. Jesus says the kingdom of God is NOW. Right this minute. One of our monks, Bonnie Spencer, speculated that that teaching, that the kingdom of God is *now*, is too heavy for us. So we fire Jesus off into the second coming. Or we make up the ascension. We may even make up the resurrection. Because the present moment is too heavy. It requires too much awareness. And monasticism, whether it's Buddhist or Christian, has always been focused on the present moment. That's what makes our life both a joy and so difficult, because it takes so much energy to remain conscious; it takes so much energy to be aware.

Andrew: It takes so much energy to love. I could have all these great hopes of heaven, and I still have to deal with all of you. And you have to deal with me. Heaven may come in the future, but the kingdom is where you have to live. The kingdom and heaven are not necessarily the same thing. If you haven't lived in the kingdom, don't worry about heaven.

John: Jesus asks Peter, "Do you love me?" And then Jesus' response to Peter's saying yes is, "Feed my sheep." Dividing the sheep from the goats, the right hand and the left hand of God, has to do with feeding the hungry, clothing the naked, visiting the sick, welcoming the stranger. Jesus is giving a definition of what the kingdom is, and the kingdom is here.

Andrew: And it's not based on right thinking.

John: No, not at all. It's based on love and compassion.

Daniel: When we had a discussion before about God and the presence of God and this constant yearning and the longing, John said that it's incredible how sustaining the tiniest glimpse can be. That also rings very true to me. It is a mystery, after all, but yet it sustains. Maybe that's the hope you were talking about.

Timothy: In the mystical tradition, the unitive moment is when you and everything else are one, like Benedict and his ray of light. The poets and saints all talk about that moment when time and timelessness, as T. S. Eliot puts it, are that one moment when it all is okay. It passes very quickly because we can't stay in that moment. Eliot says that the job of the saint is to arrive at that crossroad between time and time-lessness and to stay there. But the rest of us, we're in and out of it, and I think that one of the gifts of the practice of prayer is that we can stay in it longer. Mind you, that's not our goal; our goal is not to have that experience; our goal is the Lord. But the people who are practitioners of prayer report that commitment to prayer allows the moment to be sustained when it comes along.

Andrew: It's the beatific vision.

Timothy: The beatific vision is what Benedict had. And what's fascinating is that spirituality, theology, and science are all saying that vision is real. All is one. The cosmos and everything else are all one moment.

Andrew: I'm aware too that people hold on to what they can hold on to. We're able to sit here because of the kind of life we live, cogitating about this. But a lot of people haven't given themselves a chance or had the chance to do this. But they all have an idea. A child dying of cancer, who was in so much pain that you couldn't even touch her, said that she was ready to die, and when she got to heaven she was going to ask Jesus for a hug, because then it wouldn't hurt. I still think that is one of the most profound things that I have ever heard about heaven. It's very simple as well as childlike, but a great gift that God gives us is the ability to hope beyond our limits. Heaven in some ways is a way of open-ing up those limits, so that it's all right to think whatever you need to get you through.

Timothy: Scripture says that love drives out fear. We look at and understand the very powerful role that fear plays in the human psyche. It's no small thing. There's an undifferentiated pool of terror that everybody has, and some people more than others. What Benedict is saying, what Jesus is saying, is that love conquers that fear—not in the sense that it puts it down, but in the sense that love shows us that the pool of terror is not where we live. That is tremendous freedom: to be able to make that choice to go ahead, in the face of this terror that I might die here and still don't know what heaven is. I'm really terrified that when I die that's it.

Andrew: Or it's not.

Timothy: In Dante's *Divine Comedy,* when Dante is in hell, there is Satan frozen in a lake from the waist down. The devil can't go anywhere, can't do anything, can't create anything living or real because the reproductive organs are frozen. What the devil does create is an illusion of terror. But in fact, that's the irony. Dante witnesses this incredible suffering as he passes through the circles of hell until he gets to the dread-lord himself—and the devil's frozen. It's everybody else that's cooking. But as you follow Dante up into purgatory and paradise you see liberation and light and movement, totally different from this creature that's frozen in this lake of ice at the very bottom of the pit. That's one of those moments we're talking about, contemplating an image like this, when it all comes together and when I say, "Oh, I see."

Daniel: But what can we make of all the near-death experiences?

Andrew: It's interesting that one of the things common to all of these experiences is that people say they see light. That comes back to what we started with in this conversation.

There's a welcoming light. Now whether that means elec-
trical cycles of the brain are popping off or not doesn't matter.

Timothy: This unitive moment that you talked about, Daniel,
this glimpse—that's a near-death experience. Everything is
as it is. And if you read John of the Cross or any of the mystics, the experience that they have is what John called this
scientia super scientia, this understanding above understanding. You know it, but you can't talk about it. Just as for John
of the Cross, for people who have come back from near-
death experiences, something in their lives has changed. "I
am not afraid of dying anymore," they say, or just, "I am not
afraid." They can do something else with their lives because
they are much more "enlightened" than before.

John: I'm dealing with a friend who is near death and has
really no experience of what we are talking about, or at least
chooses not to be drawn into that experience. And I have no
idea what to do with him. He draws a profound blank when
he imagines heaven. For him heaven doesn't exist at all. I
can't imagine living without at least some hope of whatever
heaven is. It looks to me like he is living a full life, but it's
just when it comes to that moment, his own death, I think
for him there's a brick wall.

Andrew: He told me that when he was sick in the hospital,
every night he felt absolute terror. He thought he was dying.
It was absolute abandonment.

Daniel: Isn't it?

Andrew: Yes, but then I realized that I was the one who had
the hope. When I was hearing him say that, I was thinking,
"I think you are going to get a surprise."

Daniel: A big one.

Andrew: So really maybe we hold the hope for one another, even for the people like John's friend who say no. I have hope for your friend. He has brought beauty into the world. He's been a pain in the neck to the oppressors during apartheid. He's fed the hungry, clothed the naked, and so on. So, I can have the hope for him whether he has it or not. I think that's why you're in his life and why he holds on to you, John. You're his hope.

Timothy: And that's appropriate if you are a servant of Jesus—then that's who you are. You're Jesus for him. So because he's too afraid himself, maybe he's living it vicariously through you.

Andrew: We often laugh that for an atheist, he brings up God and heaven every day. If he were really an atheist, it would not cross his mind!

Timothy: I said in my sermon the week before (and I can't believe I said this out loud) that we're really called to be God. All of us are. The monastic life has always had that very mystical reality in our face all the time. Because we live in the light of Benedict's prism, this single ray of light, we're also called to become the prism ourselves. If we don't, then we've missed our call.

John: So maybe that statement by Irenaeus we sing as a Christmas antiphon is not so far off: *O wondrous exchange, Christ became a human child so that every child of Eve might become God.*

Timothy: I think it was Athanasius who said that the Eucharist is not God coming down to feed us, but God lifting us into God. Christ is calling us into God. And Christ is calling us to be Christ. Christ is calling us to return to God and be God. I love that wonderful image in one translation of Genesis: "God was walking in the garden in the cool of the evening." So God and Adam and Eve were like this. *[He crosses his fingers.]* They walked along together until Adam and Eve went in another direction and God invites them to come back and walk together.

Daniel: So would that be heaven when we walk together again?

Andrew: It's the image at the end of Revelation. Back to the garden.

Daniel: To my mind, walking together with God and, as Irenaeus said, becoming God, or being in God completes the circle with yourself as well, becoming the complete you. I have this image of another me, smiling and introducing himself to me. That person is still out there, and I am trying to get hold of him again.

Timothy: Well, the other famous quote from Irenaeus says that the glory of God is the human being fully alive. You're using the image of a circle. God's glory is the fully integrated person, when the person out there and the person that's here become the same person.

Daniel: So there you go. Heaven is a circle.

Timothy: What I find fascinating is that as we're winding down this conversation, we're still looking for an image so that we have something to say. But if we're honest about it, we could talk till it's time to go to sleep. . . .

Andrew: Till kingdom come.

Timothy: Because we'll never get to the end of it. And if we do, then. . . .

Daniel: What's next?

Timothy: That's right. Then it's just the fireworks.

CITY IN A GARDEN
Anne Harlan

"ANNIE! ANNIE, do you know where you are?" It is a
question that makes no sense. Of course I know where I am.
I am here. "Annie!" The urgent voice, mispronouncing my
name, tugged me away. It was a warm green place, with trees
overhanging a wide, smooth stream. My mother was there.

The anxious voice of the phlebotomist recalled me to a
place of high activity. Someone was telling me to breathe
more slowly; medics in leather jackets were approaching
with a wheelchair; the invasion of Iraq was still playing on
the television above my head; a police officer was trotting
next to the wheelchair; panic was coming up suddenly like
rogue waves; my husband was repeating firmly,
"In...out...in...out..." to remind me how slowly I
ought to be breathing. Much later, after all that was sorted
out and had become an event I could describe and think
about, I remembered that warm green place with the
smooth stream. I had been there before.

When I was pregnant with my daughter, I woke up one
night from a dream breathing hard, sweating, with my hands
gripping the pillow in tight fists. Just before I woke up I had
been in a narrow white-tiled tunnel being carried by a
stream of water faster and faster as the tunnel sloped more
and more steeply toward a sign at the end of the tunnel that

announced, "Dead End." I would die there. There was nothing I could do.

At the beginning of the dream I had been floating on my back in the stream, looking up at leafy branches overhanging the water from mossy banks. The stream had been broad and slow. The sky was far overhead. Light filtered through the leaves. The water carried me along gently. Gradually the canopy of trees grew closer, the stream became faster and narrower, and the surroundings closed in and became the tunnel of plain ceramic tile.

I have never been anywhere so suffused with peace and delight as that green woodsy place. Could heaven be a homecoming to that Eden from which I was expelled at birth?

I think not.

I am sure heaven is a city. Not a mere garden, or if it is a garden at all it is a public park. But surely it is a city. A city depends on movement. Traffic needs to flow in and out of it; it needs rivers, streets, meeting places. People are essential to a city, and they need to be different from each other, with different skills. Will we need plumbers in heaven? Certainly there will be people who delight in the unique properties of water. Consider the kind of person who could design the intricate system of streams and fountains in the garden of the Alhambra, or the ingenious waterworks outside the Getty Museum in Los Angeles. Just by their diversity city people can reveal to each other the infinite and various wonders of God's creation.

I used to live in New York City. What I miss most is the subway. Sitting on the subway you can consider all the ethnicities of the world as they play out in different noses and chins, different skin tones and textures of hair. When I rode the subway every day I used to play a game imagining one of the people in my field of vision without make-up, healed of any signs of ill-health or malnutrition, and wearing dignified clothes that redeemed her body and affirmed her ethnicity. The robes and crowns we wear in the heavenly choir will not make us all look the same. Our heavenly garments will be more our own than any others we have ever worn. The subways in heaven will be jammed with stunningly beautiful people, all strikingly and perfectly different. We will give thanks for an eternity in which we get to know them all.

Another game I played on the subway was surveying the newspapers people were reading. Up and down the car people were engrossed in columns of tiny mysterious characters, some in bold headlines of nonsense words, and some in lines of elegant curlicues. In what language will we greet each other in heaven? Surely the careening pitches of Mandarin will not be lost to us, nor the quick, percussive clicks of Xhosa, nor the rumbling gutturals of Arabic. Surely our resurrected tongues will be able to savor all those sounds.

About eight years ago my husband and I managed to lay aside our competitive independence and study Spanish together. We were preparing for a visit to our daughter, who was taking a college semester abroad in southern Spain. Near the end of the ten-day trip we rented a *cyclobus* in a park in Seville. We paid for an hour's rental and were off, pedaling the four-seater surrey around a network of tree-lined avenues. All feeling our own blend of relief and sorrow as our time was ending in Spain, we were behaving badly. Negotiations about whose turn it was to steer and whose turn it was to sit in the backseat where you didn't have to pedal bore the freight of ten days' triangular decision-making. But then at one point, when my husband regained the coveted steering role, the rush of freedom and power inspired him to sing out some of the Spanish phrases we had been struggling so hard to master. Soon the singing became operatic, and he slipped from Spanish into a more comfortable Italian. Careening around a corner, we met another *cyclobus,* driven by a well-dressed middle-aged couple. Having been caught singing Italian opera at the top of his lungs, my husband decided to squeeze the bulb of the clown-style horn several times and wave. After a gasp of horrified embarrassment, my daughter and I laid aside all our anxiety about respectability in a foreign culture. It became a game to see what it took to raise a smile from the staid Spaniards in the park. We sang and honked, filled with joy for the sunny day, for the orange blossoms we had smelled just outside the mosque in Cordova, for the ancient and delicate carved walls we had seen at Alhambra, and most of all for the ability to enjoy being together after all our disagreements and compromises.

What about the bitter disagreements and resentments that will inevitably trail behind each of us as we come to the gates of heaven? Never mind having merely sobbed and flung loud accusations on a public street in Granada, what about the emotional violence people lay on each other? What about our psychic disfigurements and mutilations? What about the heavy chains of our anger and remorse? We are promised that our tears will be wiped away, but not that they will never have been shed. When God wipes away the tears of genocide and child abuse, I cannot imagine that we will just snuffle and hiccup a few more times and then go wash our faces. Bellowing operatic tunes and squeezing clown horns at each other will be nothing compared to our crazy joyful antics in heaven. You can't do that kind of thing in a nice private garden, but in a cosmopolitan city people tend to let you do whatever you need to do. A friend of mine found her mother's formal funeral inadequate to her grief and ended up gathering her family at an agreed upon spot in Central Park, where on the count of three they all shrieked as loudly as they could. A few passersby glanced over at them, but no one seemed bothered by it.

I grew up in the city of Chicago, whose official motto is *Urbs in Horto* ("City in a Garden"). Although Chicago has probably been more often associated with big shoulders, political machines, and slaughterhouses, my life as a child in

Chicago centered around the verdant University of Chicago campus and a great swath of green space called the Midway Plaisance. One of my early memories is sitting on the lawn in front of Rockefeller Chapel, making a crown of dandelions for myself. On a family trip downtown to Grant Park I remember standing before Buckingham Fountain watching hundreds of plumes of water ascend in tiers toward the glorious central pinnacle well above our heads, and feeling the cool blessing of the mist on my face intensify as the breeze shifted. Imagine the glorious spectacle we'll see and the refreshing mist we'll feel standing before the heavenly fountain of righteousness.

Later in my childhood, over on State Street at Marshall Field's department store, I would ride the escalator up past floor after floor of riches, each floor large enough to get lost in. On the eighth floor I moved among towering bolts of fabric as if wandering in a ripening field, holding a paper pattern in one hand, feeling the textures of wool, terrycloth, satin with the other hand, imagining myself dressed in each of the different colors. One summer I worked with four other high school students on the staff-only floor at the top of the building, in the Interior Display department. We were allowed to help ourselves to velvet ribbons, sequins, fancy buttons, and rolls of colored felt to make ornaments for the three-story-high Christmas tree that would stand in the central atrium of the store. We were not allowed to take any scraps home with us, so the extravagant wealth of materials there made it seem like an exclusive paradise.

Furthermore, the fabled Frango Mint chocolates were made in a special kitchen on that same floor. When we had a break we would take a walk around by the kitchen, ambling casually, hoping to be offered a free sample. At the end of the week I would take the staff elevator down to a secret sub-basement where a person behind a grated window would hand me a sealed envelope with dollar bills and change in it—my reward for a job I loved anyway. By that summer, which was between my sophomore and junior year in high school, I was familiar with all the departments in the palatial Marshall Field's, and yet it was revealed to contain even more floors of riches. What wonders might there be in the other ornately graceful Louis Sullivan buildings in downtown Chicago? Or in the soaring gothic buildings of the University of Chicago? Or in other more famous cities? Let alone in God's many mansions in the heavenly Jerusalem?

One block down State Street from Marshall Field's, in front of the wide, intricately designed copper doors of what was then its chief rival, Carson, Pirie & Scott, a wizened black angel proclaimed the good news. He chanted like a street monger, repeating his proclamation over and over, drawing out the syllables at the beginning of each statement and rushing to an excited climax at the end. "Re-e-e-ead yo' Bible! Ask de La-a-a-awd for de understanin'! And He will *[big breath]* give-it-to-you!" Most of the shoppers ignored him or hustled quickly by him as if his zeal might be an infectious disease. I was a scientifically minded Unitarian child, but I loved that man.

Surely after having been given the fabulous wealth of the city in this life, our consummation with the ultimate truth will include all that. I believe we will come, in the words of W. H. Auden, "to a great city that has expected your return for years." Chicago does not expect my return, of course. Nor does New York, or any of the cities I have seen and loved. My mother has sold the house I grew up in; and my grandparents' big romantic house in Ithaca has long passed out of the family. I have no roots in any particular city. My husband and I have long hypothetical discussions about where to retire. We own no property; our families and friends are scattered all over the country and abroad. Recently, on an eleven-hour plane flight from London to Johannesburg, I agonized about the size of the world, in which love stretches us over distances that are grueling to the body. Why do we cultivate friends in South Africa of all places? To assuage the pain of physical separation I offer up my longing as a prayer. Would that my people could live together in the same city. I want to enter that City with all of them, strolling together through one of the twelve gates of jasper or lapis lazuli, chanting "Alleluia" in whatever language seems fit.

A STRANGE ROUTE
TO HEAVEN
Michael Battle

JESUS ONCE TOLD a parable to help us understand
what heaven is like. "The kingdom of heaven," he tells his
disciples, "is like a landowner who went out early in the
morning to hire laborers for his vineyard." He agrees on the
usual daily wage—one denarius, the amount needed to provide one day's food for a family—and sends his workers into
the vineyard. Since the landowner needs still more help, he
goes out again about nine o'clock in the morning. Noticing
some people who are standing idle in a shopping center, he
does something unusual—he makes an agreement before-
hand with these workers about what constitutes a normal
daily wage: "You also go into the vineyard, and I will pay
you whatever is right."

The landowner goes out again about noon, at three
o'clock, and at five. Each time he asks the same thing: "Why
are you standing here idle all day?" The usual response is,
"Because no one has hired us." Without fail, the landowner
says to all of them, "You also go into the vineyard." When it
begins to get dark, the landowner of the vineyard says to his
manager, "Call the laborers and give them their pay, begin-

ning with the last and then going to the first." This is where
it all falls apart.

Those who were hired last are paid first, and each of
them receives the usual daily wage. But when the first of the
laborers hired come to get paid, assuming they will receive
even more now that the "idlers" have been given the full
amount, every last one of them also receives the normal
daily wage. Naturally they grumble against the landowner,
saying, "These last worked only one hour, and you have
made them equal to us who have borne the burden of the
day and the scorching heat." But the owner replied to one
of them, "Friend, I am doing you no wrong; did you not
agree with me for the usual daily wage? Take what belongs
to you and go; I choose to give to this last the same as I give
to you. Am I not allowed to do what I choose with what
belongs to me? Or are you envious because I am generous?"
Jesus then sums up the parable, "So the last will be first, and
the first will be last" (Matt. 20:1–16).

Why does Jesus say the kingdom of heaven is like this
seemingly unjust landowner? I think it is because Jesus
shows us the difference between how God loves and how
we love. God's love assumes that the normal daily wage is
generosity. This is not how we normally love. Jesus requires
that we move beyond our individual concepts of retributive
justice and begin to imagine God's justice differently.
Through parables like this one, Jesus tries to get us to see the
utopian vision that results from the way in which God loves
the world—generously and without qualification. God does
not love hierarchically, the first over the last; rather, God
loves on the basis of generosity and gift. What is normative
for God is generosity.

That kind of perspective proved difficult for many of
Jesus' followers, including one of his best friends, Martha.
Martha wants her sister, Mary, to get up and help out with
dinner. So Martha is like the first shift of workers in the
vineyard. And just as the landowner surprised the first work-

ers, Jesus tells Martha to chill out and stop worrying about her idle sister. Jesus teaches a similar lesson in Luke's account of the parable of the prodigal son. So God's love looks strange—even to Jesus' best friends.

Love for God cannot be separated from love of neighbor. Jesus calls us to love God through our neighbor—by visiting prisoners, by hospitality to strangers, by actions that ostensibly give us no reward at the end of a long day's work. Jesus seems idealistic at best. When we look around and see others prospering through violence or greed, most of us pay little attention to God's love. How can we? After all, we live in a "real" world in which survival is paramount. Work with prisoners or those on death row may be typical of God's kind of love, which gravitates toward generosity and gift, but not for our kind of love that is seeking to survive in a violent world. Jesus knows our dilemma, but he does not let us off the hook. He still requires us to channel God's infinite generosity. Just as we cannot love God without loving our neighbor, we cannot worship in a church building without also ministering in a jail, hospital, or school.

God's love always points toward the capacity to love outside of self-interest. When it came to heaven, Jesus was no realist—if by realism we mean self-interest. This was his genius. Perhaps the greatest lesson in this for us is to learn that we must *prepare* to love as God loves—through random acts of kindness. We prepare through our daily prayers. We prepare through the butterflies in our stomach when we make our first volunteer visit in a jail. This kind of preparation hones our skills of navigation as we make our way toward heaven— toward the real heaven, not just our own narcissistic version of heaven. We must practice heaven. In so doing, we catch glimpses of God's idea of what's real because we are increasing our attention span to see beyond the ordinary.

The following true story helps me understand this kind of heaven. One day a young woman was invited to go rock climbing. Although she was very scared, she went with her group to a tremendous granite cliff. She mustered up great courage as she put on the gear, took a hold on the rope, and gained traction to climb the great rock. Well, she had to stop on the edge, to catch her breath. As she was hanging on the edge, the safety rope snapped against Brenda's eye, knocking out her contact lens. Now she dangled on a rock ledge with hundreds of feet below her and hundreds of feet above her! Frantically, she looked on the edge of the rock for her lens, but it just wasn't there. Eventually, her team helped her make it to the top of the rock.

At the top, a friend examined her eye and her clothing for the lens, but it was not to be found. She sat down, despondent, with the others of the party, waiting for the rest of them to make it up the face of the cliff. She wondered how she would get back down. After all, no one could make this journey for her—she had to go down herself. Then a new team of climbers met the young woman and her team. One of them shouted out, "Hey, you guys! Anybody lose a contact lens?" It turns out that an ant was moving slowly across the face of the rock, carrying the lens on its back. The young woman's father is a cartoonist, and when she told him the incredible story he drew a picture of an ant lugging that contact lens with the caption, "Lord, I don't know why You want me to carry this thing. I can't eat it, and it's awfully heavy. But if this is what You want me to do, I'll carry it for You."

I think it would do us some good to say, "God, I don't know why you want me to love my enemies, to forgive, to be generous, or to welcome a stranger. I can see no good in it and it's awfully heavy. But if you want me to love like you, I will."

The topic of heaven is important in spiritual and mystical discourse because it reorients the Western Christian imagination beyond the merely personal and individual. Among many spiritual and mystical traditions, attention to heavenly reality in the midst of earthly reality guards a sense that existence is capricious. Despite my own Western identity as an African American, I would want to encourage spiritual seekers of the kingdom of God not to give up on it. God is both at the end of our journey and at its beginning, coaxing us to realize our destination of heaven already complete in Jesus. Seeing heaven through Jesus enables sacramental realities to emerge in which our "heavenly mindedness" becomes the earth's good. Such heavenly imagination turns our attention toward justice and peace and allows us a better vision of how to live here, now, on earth.

The philosopher Simone Weil, in her essay "Reflections on the Right Use of School Studies with a View to the Love of God," discusses the quality of attention we need to develop. Whether we can maintain the proper quality of attentiveness to heaven, she remarks, does not so much depend on our penetrating God as the object of heaven; rather, our goal is to be penetrated by God. This will lead us to the final stage of the mystical way—union with God. It is only after long, fruitless efforts toward heaven that often end in despair, when we can no longer expect anything—then, from outside us, the gift of heaven comes as a marvelous surprise.

WHERE SORROW AND PAIN ARE NO MORE

Margaret Adams Parker

TO BE HONEST, I've never thought much about heaven, at least in any systematic fashion. I was interested enough to pick up, at some point, *The Great Divorce,* C. S. Lewis's allegory of heaven and hell. And I've been known to joke about my expectations that heaven had better have a comprehensively stocked art studio, as well as a fabulous bookstore.

But in looking back through many years of making art and also teaching about art at a Christian seminary, I've unearthed a great deal about heaven, although not in the expected places. I haven't glimpsed heaven among the many imagined depictions, ranging from medieval woodcuts to the visual speculations of twentieth-century outsider artists. I'm simply not drawn to "visionary" images. These are not the kinds of images I make. Instead, my image of heaven is distinctly negative (theologians would call it *apophatic*). I have no vision of what heaven is like. But I have seen, and I have also made, pictures of what heaven is not.

I am a concrete thinker, and so my art is earthbound, far from visionary. I've always understood the incarnational nature of Christianity as a charge to take seriously life in *this* world. What's more, my two great artistic mentors—Rembrandt and Käthe Kollwitz—were rarely given to visions. Rather, their work was grounded in the physical, spiritual, and social realities of life. Such symbols as they used (most notably Kollwitz's use of the skeleton to represent death) served to underscore their understanding of human existence as it is. They recorded moments as small as a child learning to walk and as momentous as war or revolution. Even when picturing the incarnation, that most heavenly of earthly events, both artists showed the miracle taking place in a tangible human setting.

Consider some of these two artists' characteristic images. Rembrandt's drawings testify powerfully to his all-encompassing interest in the life around him. He depicted everyone he saw—beggars and merchants, rabbis and serving girls—with the same probing yet sympathetic scrutiny. His drawings of his wife Saskia constitute a particularly poignant record: we watch as she endures four pregnancies, suffers the deaths of three infants, and finally dies at thirty, a short nine years after their betrothal. We glimpse her first in a silverpoint drawing (1633), made the week of their engagement. In this love poem in line, Rembrandt shows us a winsome young woman, resting her cheek lightly against her hand, dangling in her other hand one of the flowers that also adorn her straw hat. In a pen and ink drawing made four years later (1637), Saskia lies in bed, supporting her head heavily on her hand, staring out with a weary and resigned expression. And in the image that Rembrandt sketched on a tiny etching plate the year Saskia died (1642), she has become an old woman, worn, gaunt, and desperately ill.

Käthe Kollwitz's imagery is more politically engaged. The daughter of a trained lawyer who chose to work as a builder rather than practice within the Prussian legal system, she spent her life depicting the plight of the poor and protesting the ravages of war. In her first great print series, *A Weaver's Rebellion* (1897–98), she chronicled the causes,

progression, and bloody aftermath of the 1844 revolt of
Silesian home weavers against their employers. The series
begins with *Poverty* (1894), where a family of weavers gathers around the deathbed of an infant, and concludes with
End (1897), where the bodies of slain revolutionaries are
being laid out on the floor of a weaver's cabin. In both of
these dimly lit interiors, the looms and other apparatus of
the weavers' trade stand as ominous reminders of the
weavers' plight.

I would never have thought to link any of these earthly
images with heaven until I recalled Matthias Grünewald's
Isenheim Altarpiece (1511). This enormous altarpiece—eleven
feet high, almost twenty feet wide, and constructed in three
separate layers of images—manages to be simultaneously
earthbound and visionary. It contains the most graphic of
crucifixions and the most hallucinatory of resurrections. The
altarpiece was created for a hospice in Isenheim, Germany,
where members of the Antonine order treated victims of
ergotism (called St. Anthony's fire). The condition resulted
from eating bread made with ergot-infected barley. The disease was characterized by burning lesions, treated with
amputations as limbs became gangrenous, and resulted,
inevitably, in death.

While there was no cure for the disease, those suffering
from it must have found comfort in viewing the great altarpiece, which was opened and closed to reveal different
images on different days. On weekdays viewers would have
seen the outermost layer, depicting the *Crucifixion.*
Grünewald's crucified Christ is a graphic image of torment,
his flesh a sickly green and marked with lesions and thorns,
his hands and feet twisted in agony. On Sundays, Christmas,
Easter, and other feast days, the outer layer was opened to
reveal the second layer, picturing *Annunciation, Incarnation,*
and *Resurrection.* The contrast between Christ of the
Crucifixion and the *Resurrection* is arresting. The suffering
Christ has barely enough energy to draw breath; the risen

Christ is joyfully, triumphantly *alive*. Surging with energy, he raises his arms and spreads them wide to display the wounds in his hands. All five wounds radiate beams of light. Moreover, Christ's hair is washed clean and golden, his garments are shining and new, and his figure is posed against a glowing nimbus, blue on the outer edge, turning to red, and glowing golden in the center, just behind his head. But to those suffering from ergotism, the most significant feature of this image would have been Christ's flesh, which appears whole and sound, cleansed of every blemish and wound.

I have looked at this *Resurrection* countless times with my students, yet my first response is always this same: it seems unbearably psychedelic. (I am reminded of the posters from my college years of rock stars in day-glow colors.) But when I remember the context, and think of the sufferers who gazed on this image, I am always moved. To the victims of ergotism, the *Crucifixion* was a reminder that God suffered *with* them, *for* them; the *Resurrection* showed them what heaven would be like: not just a place where their sins might be forgiven but where their suffering bodies would be healed and made whole. I still don't like this image, and I don't think I will ever respond instinctively to any such vision. But the contrast between Grünewald's *Crucifixion* and his *Resurrection* enables me to understand that the earthbound image can teach us about heaven simply by showing us what heaven is *not*.

Heaven has to be a place where political repression and the casualties of war are healed. Think of Goya's *Third of May, 1808* (1814), or Picasso's *Guernica* (1937). Goya's painting memorializes the executions carried out in Madrid on that day in response to a popular uprising against Napoleon's army the day before. Goya divided his canvas between the victims on the left and their executioners to the right. The soldiers all stand in the same rigid position, their faces turned away from the viewer, their rifles leveled at the identical angle. By contrast with the anonymous efficiency of the executioners, the victims form a chaotic mass, their fear and despair transparent. The bloody bodies of the dead sprawl in a heap on one side, while from the other side the condemned trudge fearfully out of the dark night toward their fate. Between them kneel the men facing the firing squad. They pray, plead, rant, or cover their faces. The light of a huge lantern focuses attention on one particular peasant in a white shirt. He kneels, an expression of horror on his face, his outstretched arms recalling the crucifixion.

Picasso's *Guernica,* arguably the most significant painting of the twentieth century, was painted to protest the bombing of the town of Guernica in 1937, during the Spanish Civil War. The gigantic canvas—almost twelve feet high and twenty-six feet across—is filled with fear, chaos, and confusion. A man with a broken sword in one hand lies prone across the foreground; a woman screams over the dead child in her arms; another searches the wreckage, lamp in hand; another lifts her hands above her head and cries out in fear; a wounded horse shrieks in the center. The absence of color—the painting is limited to black, white, and shades of grey—calls to mind news bulletins from contemporary newspapers and newsreels. The size of the painting and the scale of the figures assault the viewer. Picasso forces us to confront the obscenity of civilian casualties (the destruction that we now describe, disingenuously, as "collateral damage").

Heaven also heals the more intimate, personal struggles of life. The pain that we see in Rembrandt's images of Saskia dying will be erased, as will the lifelong experiences of rejection and loneliness that we sense in Vincent van Gogh's great series of self-portraits. Van Gogh failed in his early ambitions to pastor among the poor. He subsequently channeled his passion and awkward intensity—qualities that so often made him seem frightening to others—into his pursuit of art. His self-portraits (over forty in all) offer painful glimpses into the artist's restlessness, intensity, and unhappi-

ness. Tellingly, the eyes which confront us in all of these
paintings are the same: anxious and piercingly sad. Indeed,
in 1890, shortly after van Gogh's death, his brother Theo
wrote about him to their mother, "Life was such a burden
to him. . . ." The artist's own words ten years earlier confirm
the immense loneliness conveyed by the self-portraits:
"There may be a great fire in our soul, and yet no one ever
comes to warm himself at it, and the passers-by see only a
wisp of smoke coming through the chimney, and go along
their way." In his final *Self-Portrait* (1890), painted just
months before his suicide, turbulent blue brushstrokes dom-
inate the background, move into the blue of his coat and the
shadows of his face. His brows are furrowed above glaring
blue eyes, his unhappiness palpable in the short, angry
strokes that model his face.

Students sometimes ask why artists make such images
and why we take time to study them, since the subjects are
so unsettling. They wonder why we dwell on these dark
aspects of life when we might focus instead on moments of
beauty, serenity, or joy. In truth, lament is a significant theme
in my own work—although students are usually too tactful
to ask the same questions of me—and I suppose this is why
I respond so strongly to the images I have described. One
early lament was a woodcut titled *ENOUGH* (1996), showing women in various postures of grief. They are silhouet-
ted against a blood-red landscape into which the word
"ENOUGH" is carved in a repeating spiral. I created this
print in response to the assassination of Israeli Prime
Minister Itzhak Rabin, who famously declared, "Enough of
blood and tears. Enough." But I resisted for five years the
impulse to add Rabin's words, along with his name, as a sub-
title. I didn't want to limit the meaning of the print to one
person or event; there are so many places and times when
we urgently need someone to cry, "Enough!" I also wanted
to acknowledge the reality that women—who must send
sons and brothers and husbands to war, who bear dispropor-

tionately the consequences of wars and displacements—are often the ones who initiate the hard work of reconciliation.

In the intervening years lament has become a recurring theme in my work. Often the impulse to make these images arises spontaneously out of my response to an event in the news: genocide in Rwanda or Darfur, violence in the Middle East, mental instability in soldiers returning from battle in Iraq. It is as though the subject asserts itself, demanding depiction in a woodcut or sculpture. In making each image I strive to enter the experience with my body as well as my heart and mind: I want the gestures of the bodies (as much as the expressions on the faces) to draw viewers into the story. This intense identification with the suffering of others is a form of prayer. And I am gratified when the resulting image, like a psalm of lament, can make visible and real the experience of the sufferer.

This happened with *African Exodus* (1997), which I created in response to news descriptions of masses of refugees fleeing genocide in Rwanda. I depicted a lone woman, carrying her possessions on her head and leading an exhausted child across a parched landscape. While it seemed presumptuous to speak about this experience out of my comfortable suburban studio, the initial sketch shaped itself on the page virtually unbidden (a rare experience), and I could hardly refuse it. I knew that the woodcut had captured some truth when, in 2001, a student from Southern Sudan chose this print to take home with him, and later, in 2004, when the United Nations High Commissioner for Refugees printed the woodcut as the frontispiece to their publication on *Refugee Children*.

One lament was unexpectedly, horribly prophetic. The image—the final woodcut for an exhibition about Jerusalem—was drawn from the Book of Lamentations. *Lamentations 1, "How lonely sits the city that once was full of people. How like a widow has she become . . . "* (2001) portrays the personification of the city as a young widow who turns from the viewer, her face hidden in her hands. As I worked, I reflected on the sad reality that these words were as apt in contemporary Jerusalem as they were twenty-six centuries ago. But text and image suddenly took on a terrible new meaning closer to home: the date was September 11, and I was carving this block when I heard, from my studio, the impact of the plane striking the Pentagon.

But lament was not always my theme. Fifteen years ago I was contentedly painting Washington cityscapes and wooded landscapes, searching for the visual poetry of light, shape, and color. Today I still enjoy the beauty of the natural world and I still make prints of fields and streams and trees. But I have discovered that these always take second place when a lament rises out of contemporary events and demands my attention. Right now I have prints in various stages of preparation: sketches of Washington's cherry trees, the magnificent Dawn Redwood from the Duke Gardens, redwood-lined waterfalls near the Big Sur coastline. But these images are stuck in line behind a woodcut about Iraq and what war does to the soldiers who must fight it.

Friends still ask me why I don't go back to making those nice cityscapes. Sometimes I wonder myself. But then I am caught up short by reports of the morgues in Iraq filling up with bodies; of dead and wounded soldiers returning to our own country; of southern Lebanon in ruins; of children in northern Israel unable to sleep for fear of incoming missiles; of global warming and environment destruction degrading the world we are leaving our children. I acknowledge about myself that I am neither a street protester nor a letter writer. I am a maker of images, and this is work I can do to bear witness to these sorrows. In this task I stand on the shoulders of artists long dead and beside artists still working.

In a very fine book, *A Theological Approach to Art* (1967), Roger Hazleton explains my motivations better than I can: "One does not go to such trouble to portray human brokenness, erosion, or malignancy unless one is deeply concerned with true and whole humanity." This truly is heaven: a place where humanity, individual by individual, is restored, made true and whole. *Deo gratias.* It is a place where human brokenness, erosion, and malignancy are healed. In heaven there will be no more war; no more oppression and degradation; no more sin and sorrow and death. In the burial office in *The Book of Common Prayer,* we recognize these expectations of heaven when we pray:

> Give rest, O Christ, to your servants with
>   your saints,
> where sorrow and pain are no more,
> neither sighing, but life everlasting. (BCP 499)

This brings me back, full circle, to Rembrandt. His etching of *The Adoration of the Shepherds, with the Lamp* (1654) is always the first work that I show new students. Light radiating from the Christ child illumines Mary's peasant face, as she lifts her cloak to reveal the infant, and Joseph's arms, beckoning in welcome. Their gestures draw the wondering shepherds into the light from the darkness outside. Even the shaggy beasts gaze toward the light from the shadows of the barn. The miracle of the incarnation is revealed out of, and by contrast with, the surrounding darkness. It is the same with my vision of heaven: out of the sorrow and suffering of this world I anticipate heaven's brightness.

HEAVEN CAN'T WAIT

Maggie Ross

"WHAT DO YOU THINK happens when we die?"

My eighty-year-old mother had the pedal to the metal. We were hurtling through spring sunshine and green hills, past the long sparkling lakes that mark the San Andreas fault just south of San Francisco. I was careful, very careful, not to express surprise at her question. Religion was an unmentionable subject in our family, a topic loaded with dangerous intimacy.

Her Edwardian outlook, capacity for denial, and inability ever to let go of anything were hallmarks of her life, yet she had grown old with unusual grace. Paradox was her *métier*: when facing a difficult choice she would worry and fret, twist and turn, her anxiety levels skyrocketing. But when the dreaded task could be avoided no longer, she would walk serenely through the jaws of whatever it was she had feared as if she were going to a garden party at the Palace of the Legion of Honor.

She liked to present herself as a *grande dame,* but she had a wild streak, which I encouraged whenever it peeked out of its elegant shell. The car we were riding in was the consequence of one of these glimpses. Little did I know that it was a mild flutter compared to the escapades her envious, more conventional friends would recount after her death.

167

"What do you think happens when we die?" Her question was costly; how long had she been waiting for the right moment to ask it? What had provoked it? She was not requesting a story or a discussion but demanding a naked truth that would bridge the abyss between our conflicting perspectives. Underneath my mother's studied nonchalance lay barely controlled terror; for me, death was as familiar as my own face.

I shifted slightly, as far as the bucket seat, restraints, and g-forces would allow, trying to respond as casually as she had asked the question, laughing a little at the existential and cosmic incongruities.

"My views on this subject are mindlessly simple. I think the universe is made of love and that when we die we are somehow drawn deeper into that love."

Having obtained the information she desired, Mother withdrew into her own thoughts, and we traveled the rest of the way to Palo Alto in silence. I have no idea what she thought about heaven. She was an obsessively private person and not an abstract thinker. Until the last four nights of her life, when she had no other choice, this single exchange was as close as she would ever allow me to come. To ask for comfort would have been, for her, a serious moral lapse.

Heaven has never been an option for me, at least not the domesticated heaven of sentimental writers, nor the judgmental "make your choice between heaven and hell" of self-righteous preachers, nor the wishful-thinking heaven of being united with "loved ones" whose subtext frequently concerns the tragic consequences of toxic relationships. Most of what I hear adults say about heaven seems uncomfortably like the stories they tell themselves when they are trying to avoid reality.

Perhaps a childhood brush with death rendered these heavens implausible. Perhaps awareness of the unrelenting squalor of post-Depression slums, or photographs of concentration camps, or the nuclear threat—any of these could have turned me off speculation about heaven.

On the other hand, I am glad that people can take comfort in ideas of after-death heaven, even people who often feel as distant from its clichéd representations as I do. One such is a friend whose beloved border collie was nearing the end of his life. Jim had been a rising star until he lost a foreleg, but his spirit remained intact. Until the end of his life he radiated the burning intensity, intelligence, and energy that is the ideal of his breed—qualities that characterize his companion and owner as well.

It was near midnight when we walked out into her cottage garden for a breath of air before bed. Stars scattered in their billions across the bowl of the sky, hanging low enough to touch, receding one behind the other to infinity, heaven and earth in a single frame. The little bear turned on its tail around the pole star, Orion pursued the Pleiades in hopeless desire, Sirius strobed its glory directly overhead. My friend asked if I knew which one it was.

". . . also known as the Dog Star because it follows Orion faithfully across the sky."

We stood there in the piercing cold, caught by immediacy, a felt sense of the starry dance. We leaned instinctively against the wind created by our small earth turning at speed through the pattern.

"Right," said my friend, suddenly, quietly, with a slight firm nod of her head. "Jim is going to Sirius when he dies."

Her words went deep.

Sirius is now the abode of all good dogs who have died (and bad ones, too, who there will come to their goodness and truth). From Sirius their loyalty and love shine down on us as they return their star-stuff whence it came. Sirius has always made my heart leap, but in the wake of that conver-

sation its presence has taken on a particular kind of glad-
ness—even as I wryly acknowledge the absurdity of this
mad mythology.

It is precisely this sort of anthropomorphizing of
heaven—but taken seriously and literally—that puts me off.
It makes no sense to talk about heaven as just another place,
no matter how wonderful. Furthermore, heaven-talk about
a god who condemns, a god I associate with the atrocities
committed by humans, is revolting. If that is who God is, I
want no part of him.

It has always been disturbing to me to see people stake
their lives on human projections they call "heaven." As time
has passed and the so-called spirituality movement has
developed, possessive talk about heaven has given way to a
more narcissistic materialism. These days, people walk
labyrinths the way their forebears clutched at magical devo-
tions. They cling to the way of images *(kataphatic),* while
protesting that the way without *(apophatic)* is too hard. They
point to enneagrams and Myers-Briggs stereotyping to justify themselves, conveniently forgetting that whatever one's
attrait, spiritual growth is a seamless dialogue spiraling ever
deeper between the images of belief and the iconoclasm of
faith.

Perhaps they have never realized that every one of us
without exception must learn the apophatic way for the
simple reason that every one of us without exception must
die. It is far simpler to learn this dispossession now through
imageless meditation and prayer, which helps us to "fear the
grave as little as my bed," as Thomas Ken's hymn reminds us,
than to wait, like Tolstoy's Ivan Illich, until the last few days
and hours of our lives.

As my mother waited.

There was a time when I thought that whatever judgment was, its standards would be tailored to the individual.
This notion probably arose from the Narnia story that suggests that after death you get what you believe—and for a

time it made me very uneasy. But ultimately I rejected it, not only because of its implicit blackmail and because I was already aware of judgment in every moment, but more significantly on the grounds that there are people who have never known anything but abuse and violence, and these are surely included in "the poor" on whom God has infinite mercy.

I had been given a taste of this mercy when I was five years old. Like all true "heavenly" encounters, it left a trace, and from the moment I returned to myself until the present moment, it has been the lodestar of my life.

But I do not think of this encounter as heaven.

On November 5, 2001, seven weeks after the attack on New York, there was a display of aurora borealis so intense it was visible as far south as Alabama. Unlike most auroral displays, which are unstable and short-lived, this one went on for hours. Here in Southeast Alaska, we could see it even before the sun was below the horizon. The entire sky turned blood red.

An auroral corona began to form, shimmering rays of every shade of crimson from the palest pink through rich king salmon to dark, dark magenta streaked with gold, all seeking a focal point.

Before the ability to verbalize deserted me, I was possessed by a longing for everyone in Washington, everyone in the Middle East, everyone planning violence and revenge to experience this overwhelming transcendence. If only they could see it, everything else would pale into insignificance. They couldn't fight, they couldn't. . . .

Then the tears began: this is why psalms are written, this is how myths are born, holy salmon guard in their flesh the light of this blessing from heaven. . . .

I went into the house, put on my warmest parka and returned to the beach.

I lay down on stones.

Around me the horizon arced two hundred degrees, a hundred miles north to south before the mountains blocked it at either end.

The aurora extended over the entire vault.

What is more, the zenith of the corona, the vanishing point at which all the rays gathered and from which they proceeded, formed above me. Cathedrals of light ascended and descended, pillars of eternity.

In some way my life ended that night. If I had turned into a block of ice while baptizing in the aurora, I would have died a happy woman.

But this was not heaven.

There was a space of about three years when circumstance created the opportunity to realize what I had always suspected I was born to do: sing the Night Office. This was not the contemporary truncated "Night Prayer" found in recent breviaries. This was full-blown broken-sleep eleventh-century Night Office with its ancient Latin chant, much of it sung from memory in the dark. We rose at midnight to pray in solitude and gathered at 1:00 A.M. We sang through the dark hours until 3:30 or 4:00 A.M., depending on the feast.

I lived from one Night Office to the next. Daytime in the scullery with carrots, potatoes, and leeks passed in a dream of fatigue and the joy of life taken out of time. Even on the mandatory night off, when I collapsed gratefully onto my bed and sank into oblivion, my heart was awake and singing.

It was neither a young community nor a happy one, but the Night Office never failed, not even when there was only one person left singing on a side during the *Laudate* psalms, the others having tranced in sleep as they leaned against their misericords. The Night Office had a life of its own, and we were privileged to be tributary to its everflowing stream. The opening of our lips immersed us in the music of creation as it sang the passing of one day and, note by note, line by line, awakened the dawn of the new. The night held all the joys and sorrows of the human race, all the agony and beauty of creation, birth, and death—named, marked, remembered, and bathed in the river of psalms flowing into eternity.

I have mostly gotten over wishing I had died in France, which process has been a greater death. The Night Office goes on, whether it is silence singing over the cold sea outside my Alaska window or Latin psalms chanted in a Provençal chapel.

But these are not heaven, either.

The wilderness here has welcomed me, and whales have sounded my bones. Sometimes my harp settles so sweetly into its tuning that alone it plays the music of the spheres. It is always trying to play, even if it risks destroying itself. That is the nature of harps.

With friends I have laughed until I cried, and alone have cried until I was empty, a tablet erased of suffering, pain, sin, joy, which together have rendered me receptive to being written on anew.

But none of this is heaven.

It was Isaac of Nineveh who confirmed what I had supposed all this time: that the biblical phrase "the world to come" refers not to pie-in-the-sky by-and-by but to "the kingdom of heaven within you."

> Once you have reached the place of tears, then know that the mind has left the prison of this world and set its foot on the road towards the new world. Then it begins to breathe the wonderful air which is there; it begins to shed tears. For now the birth pangs of the spiritual infant grow strong, since grace, the common mother of all, makes haste to give birth mystically to the soul, the image of God, into the light of the world to come.... Then you will start to become aware of the transformation which the whole nature will

receive in the renewal of all things, dimly and as though by hints.[1]

Heaven is without beginning and without end. It's when I'm not looking for heaven that heaven appears. It is by definition more than I can ask or imagine. It permeates all that I live, have lived, and will live, in weal and in woe. It suffuses the ordinary flow of our lives if only we will stop trying to cut it down to our size, to objectify it, to make it finitely less than it is.

My mother solved her problem with death by having the definitive fall, fracturing so many bones that she was caved in on one side. They could not be set, as she was too fragile to risk the slightest intervention. She was in the hospital a couple of weeks, then demanded to go home. Twenty-four hours later she was back with drug-resistant pneumonia.

I bought scrubs and a cot and moved into her room.

She was lightly comatose, parched with a high fever. There was little to be done: cold cloths for her forehead, swabs to keep her mouth moist. She sucked hard on the swabs.

The second night her fever broke, but she was awakened by pain. In her final two years she had become paranoid and after her fall had refused painkillers on the grounds that they might further weaken her failing heart.

Diffidently, I suggested that, nonetheless, a little morphine might be a good idea. She looked at me suspiciously as if she thought I might be trying to do her in, then agreed.

The bolus hurt her; she was skin and bones. I asked the nurse to put her on a drip.

The third night she seemed to rally. She was sometimes unconscious, sometimes wide awake. "Don't waste your

1. Isaac of Nineveh, translated by Sebastian Brock, in Maggie Ross, *The Fountain and the Furnace: The Way of Tears and Fire* (Mahwah, N.J.: Paulist Press, 1987).

money on skin creams," she admonished in one lucid interval. "They don't work!"

In another, her eyes flew open: "I'm getting better!" she announced in a tone of voice that brooked no contradiction.

And as an afterthought: "I've always hoped you'd change your mind, get married, and have some grandchildren. It's not too late!"

Denial dies hard. I was fifty-eight years old and seventeen years beyond a hysterectomy.

The fourth night she lapsed again into a light coma. The struggle between flesh and spirit seemed to be building to unbearable levels. In the small hours of the morning she appeared stuck, unable to accept fully that she was dying, unable to let go.

As I sat there helpless before her agony, an incongruous memory appeared. I had once borrowed a pullover sweater she hadn't worn for a dozen years and which, because of her arthritis, she could never wear again. I'd found it during a visit when I was helping her look deep in her walk-in closet for a pair of shoes. With great reluctance she let me take it. About a month later she made an agitated phone call to ask me if I had the sweater and to please send it back immediately.

This memory prodded another: the question and answer in the car seven years earlier. I gathered all my courage and leaned tentatively toward her, careful not to touch.

"Mother," I said as gently as I could. "Mother, it's all right to let go into love."

Her body gave a great start as if she were trying to sit up to stare me down, to negate my words.

Softly the melodies she had once loved to hear her husband sing began to spin from my lips. Psalms we had read at *her* mother's dying emerged from the everflowing stream to sing the dawn. Slowly her body began to relax. The strain left her face. She was going to a garden party through the jaws of death.

But now a different struggle began, one more pitiful by far than the first. It lasted the next twelve hours. She had consented to die, but her physiology was so conditioned to never let go that it fought her will and her desire for every breath and every heartbeat.

During her final hours she was no longer responsive. Her eyes were half-open, unblinking. Slowly the inexorable pattern established itself, breathing that lingered and lagged and stopped and started again after successively longer pauses. Her pulse lurched in her throat, then, after an impossible gap, throbbed again.

Suddenly, on the last beat, her face became fully conscious, alive, sentient; her features contorted with excruciating pain and effort—and in the same fleeting instant, collapsed.

In the end, it seems, the only way she could let go was to break her heart.

Heaven can't wait.

BODIES, RISING

Martin L. Smith

DANTE WAS BLESSED with Virgil as a guide to the afterlife, but I would be satisfied to get the kind of advice the fabled Irishman offered to a lost tourist: "Well, if I were going there, I wouldn't start from here!" Propose an exploration of life beyond death on the theme of "heaven" and I soon feel queasy and lost in the thickets of unbidden associations: the inane jokes about arrivals at the pearly gates, the *New Yorker* cartoons with the robed figures on the clouds, the mawkish platitudes uttered at funeral parlor viewings about our departed relatives looking down on us from "up there," the Old Master paintings crowded with angels and brocaded saints. I need a guide to give me permission not to have to believe in this place up there called heaven in which God is supposed to live, though strangely lost to view in the clutter of religious bric-a-brac that successive ages have accumulated there.

But I do have my own guide. My soul knows where it wants to start, and if that seems presumptuous I can quickly counter that impression by giving the coordinates of my starting place. It actually is on the map in the Apostles' Creed. I am proud that the church was brave enough to stipulate that we pin our hopes not on the commonplace idea of heaven, but something much more queer and rare: the resurrection of the body. Few people want much to do with that these days, so I lay myself open to a suspicion of affectation, but for me this starting place is not something I chose. Knowledge is the strangest thing, because when we really know something, our bodies seem to know it even more surely than our minds. There is a felt sense of truth, and the heart beats faster and our limbs tingle. True knowing brings arousal. I am aroused by the hope of the resurrection of the body. It is a whole-body sensation, as I felt again not long ago entering the side chapel in the cathedral at Orvieto and finding the newly restored frescoes of the resurrection on the last day. Here in the images of the amazed dead emerging from the red clay is something I know.

People may or may not want to "go to heaven." Some take the idea for granted, many are agnostic about it; others are simply unmoved. But I have never met anyone who seriously welcomes the promise of the resurrection of his or her body who hasn't undergone some kind of awakening. Through some kind of visitation we are aroused by a sense of the sheer intensity of God's desire for us. We may have had some previous sense that after death we can be "away from" our bodies and somehow "be with the Lord," as St. Paul says. But apparently God cannot be satisfied with heaven as a spiritual plane for disembodied existence. God's desire is to re-embody us for eternity.

The creed obstinately affirms that looking for the resurrection of the body is not a strange mystical speculation on the outer fringe of religion. This hope is set on the bedrock of the gospel, literally built on the rock, the one that was hollowed out for Jesus' tomb, the place where Jesus was re-embodied after death, the place where God revealed the lengths to which his desire for us will go. On Friday, Jesus had died with the cry, "My God, my God, why have you forsaken me?"; in the dawn of Sunday he came alive into the discovery that he was indeed the Beloved—Jesu, joy of *God's* desiring—and so are we.

When I was sixteen I turned a corner into my first intuition of God's desire to re-embody us. Literally, because I
came to a turning on a staircase in London's Tate Gallery
and was suddenly confronted by a vast painting, *The
Resurrection in Cookham Churchyard,* by Sir Stanley Spencer.
The painting depicts the village church at Cookham in the
south of England, where the artist lived for most of his life.
It is the Last Day, the Day of Resurrection, but there is no
apocalyptic firework display of falling stars or swooping
angels of judgment. The Last Day is a serene English summer day. All the graves are opening up, the turf peeled back
like the lids of sardine cans, and the awakening dead are
emerging, some still yawning, others looking curiously at
their neighbors. All are clothed, whether in the print frocks
of recent years, or the coats and knee breeches of past centuries—except one. At the center of the painting is a young
man with naked torso looking serenely to one side, his
elbows resting on two headstones.

I was filled with emotion and curiosity, feeling that this
figure must be a clue to the meaning of the painting. And it
is. I discovered soon after that this figure is a self-portrait of
the artist who began the picture after his first sexual experience. Now I wasn't so innocent as to be unaware of
Rabelaisian puns that exploit the resonances of erection and
resurrection, but this scene is not an eccentric allegory of
emergence into the world of sexuality. Rather the instinct of
the painter was to locate his own discovery of erotic desire,
desiring and being found desirable, in the largest vision of
God's desiring of us all, as we are, in the fullness of our
embodiment and the uniqueness of our historicity. He knew
that desire is nothing if it is not particular and embodied, so
he painted divine desire as it raises to life not humanity in
general, but the actual generations of people who have lived
and died here in Cookham, Berkshire.

Then six years later I turned another corner deeper into
the mystery. I was in Kiev, fulfilling the dream of tracing the

footsteps of my forbears. I had just been to Yalta, where my grandmother's family had their summer home at the beginning of the last century, and to the church where my grandfather, an engineer in the Imperial Navy, had first set eyes on her during the liturgy and had fallen in love. And now I was making a pilgrimage to the place where Russian Christianity had begun, to the spot where Prince Vladimir had been baptized, and to the Monastery of the Caves there which had been the center of evangelism for almost a thousand years. Beneath the monastery is a labyrinth of chambers hewn from the rock. Into these the bodies of generations of monks were laid to rest, coffinless and preserved intact through natural mummification. Turning this way and that in the caves, I finally came to a place where I could sit and rest among these dark ancient bodies patiently waiting with folded hands. Occasionally, school girls on a tour would pass by, squirming at a sight they found only macabre. I was in a very different space from them.

It seems strange to think of a catacomb as a place for the arousal of desire, for the arousal of a piercing intuition of a God who desires us, but something had happened to me in Yalta a few days before which had broken me open. I had been sitting outside that church in which my grandparents had fallen in love listening to an outdoor concert, and when it ended I began to stroll toward the seashore. I had not gone far before I sensed that someone was following me. Looking round, I saw a fair-haired man about my age who stopped when I did and then resumed whenever I moved on. As a foreign tourist behind the Iron Curtain, I felt acutely uncomfortable. What could this mean? All my attempts to shake my pursuer off failed, and once I reached the sea wall he caught up with me and started to talk with great intensity. We both tried a variety of languages—I even made a ludicrous attempt to speak in Latin—but there was none that we had in common. Finally, he concentrated his effort and gazing intently into my eyes with his hands on my shoulders, pronounced in English the words, "I love man."

The shock was in recognizing that I attracted him, that I was desired. It was the first time that a stranger had ever made me reckon directly with the force of attraction. But if this is what is meant by being "cruised," there seemed to be nothing sleazy at all about it. In just these three words, he spoke the truth about his sexuality (something as a young priest I was very wary of doing myself), and took the risk of owning his attraction to me (something I had always been too scared ever to do with anyone). But, strangest of all, the simplicity of his avowal gave it a deeply impressive, if unintended, all-embracing import, as if he were affirming a love for humanity itself at the same time: "I love man." It didn't seem incongruous to hear an echo of the way prayers in the Orthodox liturgy address God as "the lover of mankind"— *philanthropos*. The stranger and I spent an hour outside the gates of the old Tavrida hotel, talking just for talking's sake, he in what I eventually grasped was Czech and I in English. Then we reluctantly parted. It felt like one of those visitations that have made people speak of angels.

Afterward, in the caves beneath the monastery in Kiev, I felt the force of our own attractiveness to God, a God who wanted all of us and all of me, even to the extent of raising all of me from the dead. A God trying to find a common language to communicate his desire, and then putting that speech into flesh in the person of Jesus, whom he raised from the dead to show what his love intends to do with us.

Back at home, these memories continued to develop in the darkroom of my heart. *The resurrection of the body.* What does that mean? I don't believe that one day God will reassemble the elements that happened to compose our bodies on the day we died so that our soul can reanimate them. When I got back from Russia I came across a perfect example of what happens when the doctrine is literalized. The only claim to fame of our neighboring parish of

Welwyn was that Edward Young, one of the most fashion-
able of the "graveyard poets" of the eighteenth century, had
once been rector there. His ghastly verses turn the doctrine
of the creed into a gothic nightmare as

> The various bones, obsequious to the call,
> Self-moved advance; the neck perhaps to meet
> The distant head, the distant legs the feet.
> Dreadful to view, see through the dusky sky
> Fragments of bodies in confusion fly,
> To distant regions journeying, there to claim
> Deserted members and complete the frame.

Then I discovered the *Book of Hours* by Rainer Maria
Rilke. This is a cycle of poems in which the poet explores
the spiritual vision that had been opened up by his visit to
Russia in 1899, and one of its most glorious features is its
grasp of the mysticism of the resurrection of the body. The
God who is praised in these poems is not a God who dis-
cards the world as a mere temporary vale of soul-making, a
husk to be discarded when souls are released to go to
heaven. This God is infinitely receptive to creation and
embraces all of it into his eternal memory, a God who particularly delights in the new creations in which we human
beings have also played a part. The poet hails God, "You are
the inheritor," the heir of all creativity, his own and ours.
God will inherit for eternity every transient season, every
fleeting moment, the cities we have created, our poetry and
our music. And by a strange coincidence that pleased me,
Rilke includes among the places God will take up into eternity Kiev's Monastery of the Caves and its winding maze of
"darkling corridors." He evokes the lovely image of a great
fountain; the world's "superabundance," to which we contribute all the achievements of our creativity and imagination, wells up and then flows down to fill the great basin of
God's receptive memory. "Into your valleys will all their fullness roll / whenever things and thoughts are overflowing."

The freedom of the poetic imagination helped me move from thinking of heaven as a place in which God dwells as one inhabitant among others, to the vision of God himself as the space into which we will be welcomed. Heaven is a spatial metaphor for the being of God. There is room within himself so that he can fulfill his desire to make us companions of eternity, room into which to raise us after death has done its worst to us. The New Testament envisions a new heaven and a new earth to be our ultimate environment. These are metaphors for God himself, whose "body of experience" includes all that has ever been. If we return to God after death, everyone agrees we can't take anything with us. But we don't need to. It is already there in God, whose memory teems with the infinite abundance of all that has ever been in this universe, and any other there may be.

What my meditations about the resurrection of the body had driven home is that heaven brings with it the prospect of God's memory as a new environment for a new embodiment. To be in God will mean limitless access to God's total, all-encompassing, and truthful memory. Everything will be real and accessible there, an inexhaustible treasure house from which nothing has been ever lost. That is why the good news can never be less than the resurrection of our bodies. To talk of our resurrection body is the only way we can do justice to the vibrant abundance of God as our new environment. To be fully embodied in this world of ours was glorious. But God himself is an infinitely richer world than any planet could offer, and our new embodiment in the world of God's fullness must be a far greater adventure than being born here on this earth.

In the traditional scheme of Resurrection Day for humanity, the resurrection of the body is the prelude to the final judgment. Inevitably, if we believe in newly embodied life in God, the prospect of judgment opens up. To put it crudely, encountering God's memory of my life and everything and everybody with which I was connected by thought or action will expose me to devastating shocks. My memory is a rag-bag of censored fragments selected from a self-centered viewpoint and manipulated to justify myself. In heaven I will get to experience, with a shocking force I can hardly imagine, how my life was lived and experienced by God. My lies will be exposed to the truth, the deliberate gaps created by my egoism suddenly filled in with all that I refused to see, my skewed perspectives drastically realigned as I see my life now through the eyes of all the others with whom I had to do, and through God's eyes. If God raises us into the total environment of truth which is his all-encompassing memory, then of course heaven means judgment and purification.

The traditional idea of purgatory, a realm of separation from God where we could be purified before entering heaven, is as misleading as it is unneeded. It is only through our intimate union with God that we will discover through his memory the fullness of our lives, and that fullness will invade our hearts with utter joy and searing pain. Joy at recognizing all the blessings and beauties we overlooked the first time round, the depths over which we had skimmed so unaware, all that others were giving us while we stayed so obstinately ignorant of our indebtedness. We will taste all the bliss our preoccupation denied us, and our hearts will overflow with the ecstatic gratitude from which our anxiety held us back.

And searing pain. The fullness of God's memory preserves the truth of our callousness and self-destructiveness, not as an abstract record, but as part of God's own living experience as the bearer of the world's pain. We will experience the wound of knowledge, the burning awareness of our need for forgiveness, and the agonizing collapse of our illusion that evil was something that lay outside us. I will know, to use words of John Baker, a revered teacher of mine, that the hands that were holding me in existence were pierced with imaginable nails.

I say "will." Suppose we can't bear to have our stories unravel in our encounter with God's total memory. Can we hold out against it, and cling to our self-justifying version of the meaning of our life? Can we refuse to exchange our memories for those of God?

Perhaps we can, and this terrible possibility must be the kernel of truth in the human intuition that there is a hell, however corrupted that notion is by sadistic fantasies. Perhaps we can refuse our new embodiment within God and recoil from the devastating process of being remade by truth. Perhaps I will refuse to know as I am known and cling to my identity, even if that means excluding myself from the bliss of oneness with God. Hell is a symbol for our power to turn down the offer of resurrection, and the terrible consequences of our propensity to frustrate God's yearning for us. The God who is love cannot send us to hell. But we all possess a key to hell's back door, and God cannot force any of us to hand it over to him. He can only hold out his pierced hands for it. Perhaps, for all we know, hell is still vacant, but there may be millions who have not yet surrendered their keys. And so we pray for the dead, that they will.

"Hell is other people," according to a character in Sartre's play *No Exit,* and it is difficult to imagine a more aggressive contradiction of the Christian vision. The doctrine of the communion of saints affirms that heaven is other people, and the hope of the resurrection of the body affirms that those other people are no wraiths and abstractions but fully alive. When most people talk of heaven, they tend to speak of reunion with certain loved ones and imagine encounters with a chosen few they want to meet. But those great artworks of the resurrection that stir me do not lie—Stanley Spencer's resurrection paintings contain over seven hundred lovingly delineated figures. The resurrection of the body brings together everyone, including our unloved ones, the strangers. Heaven is the new embodiment of all, and our encounters will be with all, stranger and former enemy, as surely as our neighbor and kin. Our lives, transfigured within the memory of God and remembered by us in a completely new way in all their depths and meaning, will be gifts for sharing with one another. It will take eternity to exchange with one another—all of us—the meaning and fullness of our lives.

In the resurrection life, I will come face to face with the stranger who followed me in Yalta, and I will show him how, through the inventive quirkiness of God's grace, two hours in his company wove a bright and permanent thread in the fabric of my life. I shall learn how he lived and died, and he will experience through me my story with Christ. We will exchange our memories, not in their old form, but as God has transformed and expanded them. And then we will let one another go, so we can go on to encounter those we once ignored, feared, and spurned and, sharing our transfigured stories, will stay with them until we can say, "I love man" or the equivalent.

Meanwhile, heaven is in the making in this world, and I am one of its makers. My hopes mean little unless they lift the routine of today. So I want to live with the thought that my life is not only a gift now for other people, but that it will be in eternity. In my odd and short life, I take up into myself a certain time, particular relationships, just these parts of creation. They will rise in God with me. So loving what I see, and what I do, and those I meet, helps to get us all ready for surprise.

REMEMBERING THE COMPANY

Kathleen Henderson Staudt

WHATEVER I KNOW about heaven, I have learned from my prayers. I'm thinking of the kind of prayer that wells up unbidden from the gut, the heart-prayer that surprises with its energy and depth of emotion: prayer without words, whose only translation might be "Please, please" or "Please, no" or "Help me, save me!" St. Paul must have been thinking of this kind of prayer when he wrote, "We do not know how to pray as we ought, but that very Spirit intercedes for us, with sighs too deep for words."

Such a prayer came out of me in the aftermath of successful treatment for breast cancer. I was thirty-seven. My children were five and two. The oldest had just started kindergarten that fall. I had weaned the youngest only a year earlier. It was too soon to be looking at my mortality. Yet I was one of the "lucky" ones. The experts had caught the cancer early. The surgery was successful, and in the months afterward I embraced life again in relief, many in my family eager to forget the whole thing, my children too young (as we thought then) to know anything had happened.

And then about three months out, I thought I felt a lump in the remaining breast, and I plunged into my own private terror. I learned later how the fear of recurrence haunts many cancer survivors even after successful treatment, but this was new to me, and paralyzing. I kept my terror to myself, not wanting to upset husband and friends. Fighting back a panic attack, I went for a walk in the park near our home. It was one of those crisp winter days when the skeletons of the tree branches trace patterns against a chalky sky. As I walked, a prayer erupted from within me, shaping into words. I heard myself pleading with God: *Lord, we have all eternity together. But just, please, please look at this man and these children: our time together is so short, compared to all eternity. Please, keep me around for their sake, and mine!*

The lump turned out to be nothing. Nearly sixteen years later, I have had no recurrence. I can celebrate that the second part of that prayer has been richly "answered," for me, even though I grieve and protest over others, faced with mortal illness, who have offered the same prayer and not survived. I don't understand why some prayers seem to be answered and others not. But that's not what this story is about.

What it is about is the first part of that prayer: *Lord, we have all eternity together.* How did I know that? What difference has it made, to find that I already had in me what we call "the hope of heaven"?

I now know that an early glimpse of what my prayer called "eternity" came on a Sunday in November while I was still in college. This particular Sunday was a festival day: the Sunday closest to November 1, All Saints' Day. I was hesitant about this celebration because it seemed so Catholic to me to speak of saints—I was raised a Presbyterian and this was an alien language. Yet I had come to love this congregation and its practices. I looked forward to the entrance of the choir in procession, at the start of the Sunday service, recognizing the faces of the "real people"—people who actually lived and worked in Northampton, had families and a life outside of the college world. I had come to know and love

these people from our weekly gatherings, whether or not I
knew their names. Their presence was part of what made the
place a home for me, just as the familiar faces in the choir
of my childhood church had made me feel at home. The
gathering of the congregation and the entrance of the choir,
ordinary people, vested, singing, and following a proces-
sional cross, told me I was part of something larger, connected to a community in ways I could not name or
articulate. The connection was the point of being there.

The children's sermon spoke to me that particular All
Saints' Sunday. Talking to the children that morning, our
preacher pointed to the words that introduce the singing of
the Sanctus in the celebration of Eucharist:

> Therefore with Angels and Archangels, and with all
> the company of heaven, we laud and magnify thy glo-
> rious Name; evermore praising thee, and saying,
> Holy, Holy, Holy. . . .

"Whenever you hear that prayer," he said, "wherever you are
in life, *remember the company.*" He meant the company of all
faithful people, those who are alive and those who have
died, who have carried the faith. He meant the people we
knew, people we admired, and with them the glorious, mysterious—and in that moment, suddenly real to me—spiritual presences: angels and archangels, and all the company of
heaven. In what he said, "saint" had nothing to do with
unusual goodness or miraculous powers. To be a Christian,
it seemed, was to be a part of the company. We were all
saints.

"Remember the company." Remember that you are part
of a great fellowship of believers, praising God, serving
God's purposes. Remember that this goes on always and forever, in this life and in the life to come. In fact, it's all one
life—and the boundary between the living and the dead is
a thin one. They are here with us all the time, seen and
unseen. This is what I heard, and what has stayed with me:

the invitation to "remember the company," to live in the
mystery, and always to dwell on the boundary between this
life and "the life of the world to come," participating in
something far greater than ourselves. That connection with
a long tradition of Christians ultimately made a catholic of
me, solidifying my commitment to a liturgical tradition
attentive to mystery, worship, and witness.

That was my first glimpse of eternity, and the second
came in graduate school. A quirky tradition at the Episcopal
church at Yale in those years was the All Hallows' Eve procession around the campus. On Halloween night, to the
accompaniment of bagpipes, clergy and students formed a
liturgical procession, dressed in albs and following a proces-
sional cross. We remembered by name our favorite poets,
mentors, and saints from the past, including them in the
chanting of the litany of the saints. Following in our train
were Yale students in Halloween costumes, making a party
of it all. Someone overheard one of them exclaiming, as we
prayed, "You know, I think these people are serious!" It was
serious play, celebration in all senses of the word. We were
participating in a mystery greater than ourselves, yet in
familiar surroundings and in festival mode. Even the cos-
tumed students helped us in that procession to "remember
the company."

Two glimpses of eternity. Now jump ahead fourteen
years to the time of my private terror. Again it is All Saints'
Sunday, and I am one of the mothers in charge of the pageant; now the procession, which I have helped to design,
includes my own children. I am just resurfacing from the
first few disorienting early years of babies and toddlers, and
a complicated move to a new community. I signed up to
help with this pageant as a way to get connected.

But what I thought was a new start is now shadowed by
the cancer diagnosis I received two weeks ago and my coming surgery. Like many facing cancer treatment, I have kept
this a secret from most people, as if, somehow, controlling

who knew about it could give me greater control over the
unknown outcomes. Very few people at church besides the
clergy know what is happening to me. As I stand with the
children in front of the church, I am not available to the
promise I once found in "remembering the company." No,
I am walking through this ritual, showing up only because I
promised to be there. I am numb and scared, vividly aware
of my own mortality. The future is a blank to me.

The All Saints pageant ends with the congregation
singing the traditional children's hymn "I Sing a Song of the
Saints of God." The words are quaint, Edwardian, a little
trite, perhaps, but they are part of the ritual:

> You can meet them in school, or in lanes, or at sea,
> in church, or in trains, or in shops, or at tea,
> for the saints of God are just folk like me,
> and I mean to be one too.

A silly song and a tall order, I reflected, to be a saint, to
believe that the saints are folk like us, and yet part of the
company of heaven. Then, through my daze of worry and
self-occupation that particular day, I recognized someone
else in the congregation who had recently been through the
surgery that I was facing. Netta, a woman closer to my
mother's age, had had a mastectomy and begun chemotherapy three months earlier. Today she was back in church,
sporting a wig and obviously glad to be there, singing out
with unmistakable vigor and joy. She looked well, she
seemed to be recovering, and she was *there*. In her presence,
in her body, she held out hope to me, even though we had
never spoken and she knew nothing about me. I had been
preparing to leave life behind—to become a ghost in the
twilight zone of hospitals, biopsies, and an uncertain prog-
nosis. By her presence Netta showed me that day what it is
to be a saint: to embrace fullness of life in the face of mortality. *"The saints of God are just folk like me,"* she sang with
the congregation, *"and I mean to be one too."*

I saw her again a few months later, after my surgery, my panic, my prayers in the park. She was participating in the joyful procession that comes at the end of the Great Vigil of Easter, the night service that ushers in the mystery of the resurrection with psalms and candlelight and ancient ritual. Then comes the first Eucharist of Easter with all the light, music, and joy a congregation can summon, singing together, in the middle of the night, "Jesus Christ is Risen Today."

As I watched that procession from the pew, I remembered the company. Once again a prayer poured out of me, in words I did not expect, in thankful, rueful laughter. *"Okay, Lord,"* I said, feeling surrounded by a sense of insistent, laughing presence. *"I see it now. Okay! So* this *is what we mean—"the communion of saints, the forgiveness of sins, the resurrection of the body, and the life everlasting."* I knew for sure, in that momentary illumination, that the life everlasting had already begun for me. It had nothing to do with my goodness or my sinfulness, or with how long I had to live the life I knew. Eternity was simply the reality at the heart of life, the reality our rituals point to and, every now and then, reveal. Netta's presence in that procession invited me to join a community that had been beckoning all along, gradually drawing me in—an eternal community, of which this particular congregation and place was a local embodiment. I knew, watching her, that by the following year I too would be part of that procession and many more like it.

What difference does it make, this perception that the life everlasting has already begun? First, it knits us together with others who have claimed the promise. Remembering the company, I also remember that the hymn they sing includes the words "Heaven and earth are full of your glory." I see, with Gerard Manley Hopkins, that "the world is charged with the grandeur of God." In Eastertide of that first year following my surgery, I remember walking joyfully through the same park with my almost-three-year-old, after we left her brother at the school bus stop, watching the tiny white violets we call spring beauties begin to open to the sunlight. I was glad to be there, embracing this life and recognizing it, in moments and flashes, as a life woven through with eternity. In the growing balancing act of those child-rearing years there were always moments of wonder. The three-year-old twirling and blowing bubbles in the summer twilight, children playing in the backyard on swings, their growing excitement as they grew older and learned to write, and read, and ask new questions about the world. I embraced parties and gatherings of the people I loved most, from the nightly dinner table to holiday traditions and reunions, festivals and processions. All these seemed to me to be intimations of beatitude, moments that made it hard to believe heaven could be better than this. Moments that say, "But there is more. More than you can imagine." I began to write poetry, trying to catch in words these moments of wonder as well as the pain of loss as they passed. As I wrote, I looked more deeply at the world, knowing that for me, eternal life had already begun.

Meadows, with their variety of flowers, shapes, sounds, and colors, came to life to my eye. So did the dunes along the side of the ocean, on our beach vacations, from the bayberry and rugosa rose of Cape Cod beaches to sea oats and wild mustard on the Outer Banks of North Carolina. In the meadows and on the dunes I observed, fascinated, how each individual stalk and flower bent in the same direction, even in a faint breeze, as if drawn to an unseen presence. Always a lover of literature, I rejoiced that other poets had seen something like what I saw. Dante represents the beatific vision in paradise as a vast rose, with the saints as the individual petals, all turned joyfully toward the heart of Love; for me the dune grasses in summer, the meadow flowers and reeds in all seasons, invited me to remember the company—the multiplicity and diversity of life and personality, held together at the heart of creation, all bending one way in response to the

Spirit of God. I revisited a little book called *The Practice of the Presence of God* by Brother Lawrence of the Resurrection, and recognized with wonder Brother Lawrence's experience of seeing a flowering tree and being overwhelmed with an awareness of the providence of God. I read with recognition the writings of Evelyn Underhill, resonating with a spirituality at once mystical and practical. All these insights came in flashes, and departed as quickly, but as the years unfolded and the children grew I came to recognize the most treasured moments of life as intimations of eternity, foretastes of beatitude. Without knowing, as I noticed and paused over the world around me, I was praying.

Sometime later, I learned that the same young priest who had preached the children's sermon at the church in Northampton so long ago in my college years had died from melanoma. A friend from church brought me a brief article Bob had written called "Cancer and God." I had not seen him since shortly after my graduation, nor did I know how his career in the church had unfolded. But once again he spoke to me—and to my praying companions, through the invisible web of prayer that we had joined. Admitting that he was shattered at first by his diagnosis and acknowledging that his disease could be treated but not cured, Bob pleaded with us all to turn aside from conflict and celebrate our common identity as brothers and sisters of Jesus.

"Our actions—our lives—matter so much," he wrote. "We can live our lives, as St. Paul would describe it, circumscribed by momentary affliction or we can recognize even in the present hardship or confusion or disappointment the preparation for an eternal weight of glory beyond all measure. You matter. Your actions matter. Will you—with me—live your life in that hope?" Bob is now a part of that invisible company of heaven that his preaching taught me to see. He died young, well before his fiftieth birthday. Coming across his story and his words in this way, five years after my own surgery, and probably at about the time of his passing, reminded me again how thin the boundaries are between the living and the dead, and how we are knit together, as one of the prayers for All Saints' Day puts it, in the mystery of God's love.

This experience of prayer as a knitting-together, a dynamic interweaving of mortal and immortal, human and divine, is the closest I have come to imagining heaven. It was expressed in that very first prayer that burst out of me: *"We have all eternity together."* But it was also part of my passionate desire to stay in this life. That's what my prayer was telling me. That is the mystery I continue to live.

Sometimes at prayer I imagine myself in the presence of all people I have encountered and whose witness has been important to me, both living and dead, those whose works I've read and those whose presence has inspired me: I think of Evelyn Underhill and Brother Lawrence; of Bob, Netta, and all the people in all the processions and congregations I have been part of; of my father, now gone on, and those in my family who still live and thrive in this life. All these faithful witnesses accompany me and whomever I am holding in prayer. I imagine us all connected to each other and yet distinct—as if leaning, like the meadow flowers or the sea oats by the Atlantic, toward a mystery that draws us all. Those who have gone before us see face to face. The rest of us remain unable to imagine heaven, and yet we are still leaning, moved by the same breeze, drawn by the same mystery. We are all bending the same way, together.

SWEET RELUCTANCE
Phyllis Tickle

I'M AN OLD MOUNTAIN girl...or back where I came from, that is what they would call me now, were I to still live there. Mountain girl, born and bred. Appalachian through and through. Of course, I haven't lived in Appalachia or any other place even approximating it for well over half a century, which tells you also that I am hardly a girl, wherever I may happen to be. But if I were home, I would be an old mountain girl until and if, by the grace of God, I should chance to live another decade or so into my mid-eighties and become either a crone or an old mountain woman, depending on how well I had aged. That's how they do it at home.

Or that's how they do it at home so long as we all understand I am referring to Appalachia when I say "home." The truth is, and always has been, that the mountains and I never had much personal experience with each other. My life, for those first seventeen years of it, was firmly planted in the buildings and lush grounds of the university where my father held sway as the dean (and this during a time when there was only one dean per university, and when the one there pretty much ran the place internally, while the president took care of external, far less glamorous matters like funding and public relations). That was home...those marble-floored corridors, the book-burdened shelves, the smell of polishing wax, the light always dimmed by thick walls and tessellated windows, the chronic low hum of papers being moved about...yes, that was home.

But as I say, it has been almost six decades now; and for over three of those decades, Sam and I have lived here. Lived in a 1950s split-level that must have been quite the cat's meow in the beginning, but is now the comfortably down-at-the-heels farmhouse that we and our years here have made of it. Of course, the house itself, familiar and disheveled as it is, is not home, even though we refer to it that way. Indeed, "Come on, we have to get on home," when we are in town and Sam says it to me, means not the house per se. In fact, it doesn't even mean the farm which surrounds the house. It means something closer to the whole little cul-de-sac of life and living that is the small, rural community where the house and the farm are. It means Lucy, Tennessee—she of the lovely name and graceful, tree-lined roads, and of quiet ways filled with cows and ponds and decaying barns.

It amuses me, from time to time, to hear our adult children refer to Lucy as "home" in much the same way that it amuses me to hear Sam refer to the Appalachia of our youth as "home." What amuses me more—or perhaps just arrests my attention every time they do it—is to hear our grandchildren refer to Lucy as "home," though by that they no doubt mean a different thing. They undoubtedly mean that same place/thing/way of being that I mean when, to this very day, I still refer to the place where my father grew up as "home." Tucked high up into the most northwest corner of Tennessee, just at the confluence of the Ohio and the Mississippi, "home" was a bawdy river town as poor as its itinerant workers and as wealthy as its cotton barons and whiskey-dealing gamblers. I loved it. It was home. He would say, my father to my mother, "It's time for us to go home for a few days," and I could see the dark river water lapping away at the foot of Main Street and smell the coal oil of the lamps and hear the singing in the fields before we ever packed the first suitcase to go home again.

All of which is, of course, by way of saying that I don't know what home is, while at the same time asserting by example that I absolutely know to the core of my being what home is. Home is a memory of what I came from; but it is so only when it is not busy being the context of my father's work and essence... or, of course, when it's not just as busy being the place where I exist or the one I spend half my time thinking about, fussing over, and attending to... or when it's not blatantly and obviously, even to me in my most unromantic moments, a state of mind... or when, at the end of a wearying round of travel, it is not the goal, the whole complex of comfort toward which I yearn.

Heaven is a lot like home; and the futility of trying to define home is frequently employed as a comfortably earth-bound analogy for the impossibility of defining heaven. I have no problem with that—with saying, and then scrip-turally validating the claim, that heaven is absolutely a place. Nor do I quibble with those who say it is internal to each of us, a prize of the heart toward which we move and yearn. I can agree that heaven is a state of being that we have not yet attained but are training to occupy, or even that it's one we remember, like Wordsworth's children trailing clouds of glory behind them as they enter physical life. I don't even balk too much at those of my friends who insist heaven is a metaphor, or at least I try to remain quiet until they have a chance to explain what "metaphor" means to them in the context of heaven-talk. I've even read some complicated histories of heaven that are very impressive pieces of writ-ing despite the fact that, in the end, their authors almost always confess to not knowing where heaven is or even whether, and in what state of being, it is. That irony does not prevent me from enjoying their commentary; nor does it keep me from being pleasurably engaged by all the essays about the history of heaven that one evokes simply by Googling "heaven," which, by the way, is a truly lovely exercise for the casually curious.

My intention, then, when I was asked to write an essay about heaven was to talk about home and about its utility as an explanation for why we have a solid half-dozen or so differing definitions of heaven, every one of them defensible and doctrinally certifiable and a few of them mutually exclusive. I even chastised myself over the course of several months for being too spiritually and/or intellectually lazy to grapple with that thorny half-dozen and come forth with what I myself really believe about heaven, with what I understand it to be. Please understand, I didn't entirely fail in this exercise. For instance, I am very sure that so long as we are caught in time—and perhaps within the other dimensions of our existence, though I tend to think time is the restricting barrier here—so long as we are caught in time, we will never be able to see heaven, which I believe is entirely and absolutely seeable.

But having arrived at that statement (which, alas, I have discovered is the only definitive one I can actually make at this juncture), I immediately run up against the very core of the problem for me: namely, that I have had what is now euphemistically referred to as a near-death experience. In 1955 when I was having it, there were no easy terms for such, no almost jocular NDE abbreviations to lessen the outréness of the experience.

The whole thing was fairly straightforward, really. I was threatening to miscarry our first child; and the drug I was given, while hardly experimental, was nonetheless new and, as it turns out, highly toxic to some women. Six or seven of us died, in fact. I didn't.... Correction: I did, but I came back.

The second most vivid memory of my life is that of sitting, hunched up like a gargoyle, in the upper corner of my hospital room, watching Sam and the nurse beat on my body, trying to restart my heart. The most vivid memory is when the corner opened up and let me out of the room into a tunnel, pleasantly grassed even on its curved surfaces. Walking through it, I could see the light coming from the other end and I could know myself drawn without effort toward That Which Waited There.

I never left the tunnel, though I stood at the edging place where it ceased and the translucent goldenness began. We talked there, just on the brink of the entering, I saying I needed to go back, that there were children I wanted to have before I came . . . and the What Is saying, "Go," and my soul breaking within me that I was leaving a greater love for a lesser one, but knowing that I must go . . . and knowing as well that I would return and that the What Is and I were, and would be, when I do return.

So it is—and for over fifty years has been—that I cannot, in any discussion of heaven, get beyond the verge where the end of the tunnel met the That Which Waits There. Neither my mind nor my necessity are ever sufficient to push beyond that place.

I do not know—none of us does—what it must have been like to have a dead man materialize through the wall of a meeting room and lay out for public viewing the holes in his hands where his executioners had nailed him to a cross or the rip in his belly where they stabbed him open to hasten his demise. Whatever they felt or experienced, those witnesses to the unspeakable, they knew. They knew what they had seen, and it was enough to persuade them at all costs of the actuality of the thing . . . which is by way of saying that I, too, know what I saw and am persuaded, at all costs, by the actuality of the thing.

I know no more to say or write; but the exercise of having tried has not been entirely wasted. At least I can admit

now that I shall never be able to speak of the what-I-don't-
know that lies beyond the what-I-do-know. There is relief
in that, as well as comfort and a certain inexpressible pleasure in realizing that someday soon I shall be about the business of greeting again that which I once left with such sweet
reluctance.

AN UPSTAIRS/DOWNSTAIRS CONVERSATION

Donna Schaper

WE KNOW SO MUCH about earth, and so little about
heaven. Educate us, O God. We know where we are from,
but we don't know where we are going. We know we came
from You and we know we return to You, but where *are* You?
Keep us from overusing the word heaven! "For heaven's
sake." "This chocolate is heavenly." Keep us from talking
with slippery metaphors about our destination and Your
home. Educate us. Keep us from putting You in an otherworldly box and also keep us from a crass worldliness. Find
a way to point our eyes upward, intelligently, with grace and
hope. Free us from captivity to these few years we have on
earth. Prepare us for the time to come. Let us know what
heaven means. Break into our fuzziness about eternal rest
and heavenly home and give us a glimpse of the reality of
our eternal future.

Some say that the only way to get into heaven is to have
a letter of recommendation from the poor. Is that true? If so,
how do I get one? Is it easier for a camel to get through the
eye of a needle than for a rich man to get into heaven? If so,
I need a lot of help. My bank account is full.

My father is in heaven, I think. But I don't know. My friend Judith is in heaven, I think, but I don't know. Roger is there, I think, but I don't know. How could I know? Am I wrong to want to know? Is my inquiry about them or about me? What happens when our last breath is drawn? Where does all that life in us and others go? Is there a breath transfer station? If so, how long do we have to stay there? Are we still *we* then or is who we are gone into a great identity composting bin? Help us to understand. Don't make fun of our questions. We know they are primitive.

Now we see in a glass dimly, then we shall see face to face. "When I was a child, I spoke like a child. . . . When I became an adult, I spoke like an adult." Does that mean heaven is post-adult? Is there such a time? Will there be any children in heaven? Forgive the dumb questions. Is there childhood, adulthood, and heavenhood? I want to know. I want to see You face to face.

Surely, our days are numbered—by birth, baptism, confirmation, marriage, death, and all the birthdays in between. Surely, our breaths are numbered by what moments we allow ourselves breathtaking experiences. Thanks be to you, Great Numberer, for the days we have. Let us know if we get a new number in heaven . . . or if numbers become irrelevant when time puts on its eternity dress.

We live day by day by day. We live very large lives in very small ways. We know our time is brief and so we are surprised at the audacity of gloom. How dare we be down in the few days that we have! Gloom we always have with us. Joy requires tending. Tend in us joy—and let us tend it in others. Dispense the gloom easily and puff it away, then breathe in the joy. We know what money can't buy. It can't buy you love, and it can't buy you joy, and we want both. Empty us so that we can be filled with good things. Let nothing be wasted on us. Let us live with heaven knocking on our door and heaven beating in our heart and death being no stranger to us. Let this knowledge of limits breed in us limitless joy—and keep gloom's audacity from ruining even a second.

In Jeremiah 33:5 You say, "I have hidden my face from this city." Ouch. What if we don't get to see You? What if You get so angry that there is no heaven, not in our city or any city? What happens to heaven if there is a nuclear war? Or global warming? Do these abdicate the promises? What makes You hide your face? Is that the denial of heaven or just a temporary pout? How long, O Lord, will You/do You stay angry?

Psalm 13:1 says, "How long will you hide your face?" Will I care about time in heaven? Will You still get mad about what is going on down on earth? Is up and down the right language? Is up down and down up? What about all the people who say earth is heaven and heaven earth? What about the great lumping of all things, as in the incarnation? Dare I expect to see Your face on earth? Or just in heaven? Or neither? Do you have a "face," O God?

If there are stones in heaven, let me pick up one each day. Let it be one that no one else has yet touched. Let me touch the stone with my warm hand and remember life in body with great gratitude. Let me steal the cold from the stone and open my heart to a new generosity, a melted insecurity, a warm hand that refuses to go stale on life, even in the afterlife.

In Numbers 6:25 we are given a prayer: "The Lord make his face to shine upon you." Oh, yes. Please shine on me. Let me shine because You shine on me. Let me know this great shining today. I can't wait till later.

Will I have time to think in heaven? Why am I so lucky and others are not? Grace me with an explanation or two, Blessed One. Point me in luck's deeper direction, that road called gratitude. I got picked up by blessing. Others were passed by. Why, Mighty God? Isn't there enough luck to go around?

When I get to heaven, please let me bring my resume with me. And if not, assuage my status anxiety, my addictions, my hunger for applause. Grace me with things that I will be able to love as much as I love each of these.

In Deuteronomy 5:4: "The LORD spoke with you face to face." Wow. I hope I get an appointment or two with the Lord. Face time, we'll call it. Apparently some people get this walk on earth. I never have. I'd like to. But I will also await heaven and walking the walk and talking the talk.

Will I be able to give gifts in heaven? Will there be birthdays? A friend once asked me to carry mangos from her Florida tree to Minnesota for her son. She engaged me once again with the power of the personal gift. Who wants something with a ribbon on it from me today? I have beautiful things to give. They are everywhere. Let me give them. In fact, bug me and urge me to give them. Let me not get stuck in a backup of gifts but instead let gifts flow from me to others. I may not be able to go shopping in heaven!

Heaven keeps driving me back to earth. Why?

Regarding the ascension and the resurrection, You may as well know. I don't get it. Why privilege up over down? Why do we sing Christmas carols about the "Joy of heaven to earth come down" and then lose it, in a violent death, followed by a preposterous rising? I thought You were a fan of earth, O God. What's the deal?

Many of us at the end of life feel like we have fished all night and not caught a thing. We are tired. We are worn. Sometimes we are just plain bored. We imagine ourselves unlucky. Grace us today with an explanation or two, Blessed One. Let us live in the land that is the opposite of fate, the land where we take responsibility for what we do and don't do—and where we leave the rest to you. When we are ready, help us cast our nets on the other side.

Help me know, Great Gift Giver, how to understand this elegant universe, with its quacks and its jaguars, its Lexus and olive trees, its ten or eleven dimensions, its wriggling strings, its deep black notes, and membranes, where waves act as particles and particles as waves, where only the seers and sages write books with titles like *The Universe in a Nutshell*. Help me understand your majesty and why you think people who have fished all night and caught nothing can still learn to fish. Help me understand why you stick with us, when and as we so miserably fail you and ourselves. Give me just a nutshell of an explanation, so that when my feeble DNA joins the majesty of the cosmos I can at least understand why my genes came together and why they then died, leaving a genetic legacy to others. Give me just a little hint.

Pascal decided to believe in you, O God, because he thought that even if You don't exist, it is equally possible that You do exist. Why not take the bet on faith? As we go through this holy time, we don't really know what all we believe or don't believe. We don't really know which part we play in the great Risen Body of Christ. We don't really know our true vocation or what we're supposed to do today. But we are a people willing to take a chance: We take our chance on you. Assign us a part; give us a role. Let us play it with vigor. Let us join Pascal in wagering on heaven. What do we have to lose?

We can't know heaven if we can't experience it! No wonder what we say about it is often so dumb. Experience is something you don't get until just after you need it. Give us the experience we need when we need it. Give us the know-how we need when we need it. Keep us from making the same mistake more than three times—and transfigure us into people who don't throw away experiences so much as use them. When we get a sniff of heaven on earth, let us mine the experience for all it is worth.

When life is too hard for us and decisions too full of risk, help us to refuse to wash our hands of it, like Pilate. Keep the basin of water away from us. Let us be the people who don't walk away, don't wash our hands, aren't afraid of life and its complexity. Let us be risk-tolerant as opposed to risk-averse. Will we still have to make choices and decisions on the other side?

Let my obsession with heaven not redeem me from the fear of hell, on this side and the other one. Let me not be naïve about evil but instead know its name and its consequences.

For an Easter card to my beloved I said, *Easter joy to you: May you find a miracle made in you and of you.* May my threshold capacity increase the closer I get to death and the open door to heaven. May I see the door open slowly when I pass. May the twilight be pretty. May it be like a miracle.

Help me to love the place where I live. Help me to understand the billions of years before me and the billion coming after. Help me understand how large and small, both, not either, I am.

Will there be hammocks in heaven? Everywhere I go in the summer I see hammocks hanging—with no one in them. Unused hammocks are a big problem in my neighborhood. So is unredeemed rest. Will those of us who don't know how to rest be able to rest in heaven? If so, I can carry on a while longer here. You also need to know that some of us like motion. Some of us even rest in motion. I hope we won't have to lie down all the time.

O God, Risen Jesus, hear our order for breakfast. We want the broiled fish and to find ourselves "strangely warmed."

LIST OF CONTRIBUTORS

MICHAEL BATTLE is a theologian and author of several books, including *Reconciliation*, a study of Desmond Tutu's theology of *ubuntu*. He teaches at Virginia Theological Seminary in Alexandria, Virginia.

AMY BLACKMARR lives in South Georgia, where her essays and public radio commentaries have earned much critical acclaim. Her books include *Going to Ground, House of Steps*, and *Above the Fall Line*.

CYNTHIA BOURGEAULT is an Episcopal priest, contemplative, retreat leader, and the author of several books, including *Love Is Stronger than Death, Mystical Hope*, and *Centering Prayer and Inner Awakening*.

MALCOLM BOYD is poet/writer-in-residence at Los Angeles' Cathedral Center of St. Paul, and is the author of thirty books, including *Are You Running with Me, Jesus?*

MARGARET BULLITT-JONAS is an Episcopal priest and the author of *Christ's Passion, Our Passions* and *Holy Hunger*.

BARBARA   CAWTHORNE   CRAFTON   is   an
Episcopal priest and spiritual director whose many books
include *The Sewing Room, Yes! We'll Gather at the River,
Mass in Time of War,* and *Let Us Bless the Lord.*

NORA GALLAGHER is the author of a novel, *Changing
Light,* and of two memoirs: *Things Seen and Unseen: A Year
Lived in Faith* and *Practicing Resurrection.*

ADDISON HALL is rector of St. Andrew's Episcopal
Church in Wellesley, Massachusetts.

ANNE HARLAN is a book artist and an elementary
school librarian in Washington, D.C.

PETER S. HAWKINS is Professor of Religion and
Literature at Boston University and the author of *Dante: A
Brief Introduction, Dante's Testaments,* and *The Language of
Grace.*

ALAN JONES is the dean of Grace Cathedral in San
Francisco and the author of many books on the spiritual life,
most recently *Common Prayer on Common Ground: A Vision of
Anglican Orthodoxy.*

THE MONKS OF MARIYA uMAMA weTHEMBA
MONASTERY live near Grahamstown, South Africa, and
are members of the Order of the Holy Cross, an Episcopal
Benedictine community.

RICK MOODY is the author of several novels, including
The Diviners, Purple America, and *The Ice Storm,* as well as two
story collections, *Demonology* and *The Ring of Brightest Angels
Around Heaven.*

BENJAMIN MORSE is a doctoral student in Old Testament at the University of Glasgow, and also writes and illustrates children's Bibles.

ROBERT A. ORSI teaches at Harvard University. His prizewinning books include *The Madonna of 115th Street; Thank You, St. Jude;* and most recently *Between Heaven and Earth: The Religious Worlds People Make and the Scholars Who Study Them.*

MARGARET ADAMS PARKER is an artist and sculptor. Her woodcuts are published in *Who Are You, My Daughter? Reading Ruth through Image and Text* and her sculpture *Mary* is in parishes around the country. Links to all of the images discussed in this essay may be found at www.margaretadamsparker.com.

MAGGIE ROBBINS is a poet, collage artist, and psychotherapist. Her novel in verse, *Suzy Zeus Gets Organized,* was published in 2005.

MAGGIE ROSS is an Anglican solitary who writes regularly for the journal *Weavings.* Her several books and translations include *The Fire of Your Life, The Fountain and the Furnace, Pillars of Flame,* and *Seasons of Death and Life.*

DONNA SCHAPER is the senior minister of Judson Memorial Church in New York City, a journalist, and the author of many books on spirituality, including *Sabbath Keeping, Calmly Plotting the Resurrection,* and the forthcoming *Living Well By Doing Good.*

MARTIN L. SMITH is senior associate rector at St. Columba's Episcopal Church in Washington, D.C., and the author of *The Word Is Very Near You, Reconciliation, A Season for the Spirit,* and *Compass and Stars.*

KATHLEEN HENDERSON STAUDT is a poet, critic, teacher, and spiritual director, and author of *At the Turn of a Civilization: David Jones and Modern Poetics* and *Annunciations: Poems Out of Scripture.*

BARBARA BROWN TAYLOR is an award-winning preacher who teaches religion at Piedmont College and Columbia Theological Seminary. The author of several books and collections of sermons, her most recent work is *Leaving Church: A Memoir of Faith.*

PHYLLIS TICKLE is one of the foremost commentators on American religion. She is the author of many books and articles, including a trilogy, *The Divine Hours,* and a memoir entitled *The Shaping of a Life.*

SUSAN WHEELER is the author of four books of poetry and a novel, *Record Palace.* The recipient of a Guggenheim Fellowship and the Witter Bynner Prize for Poetry from the American Academy of Arts and Letters, she teaches at Princeton University.